Building Family Values

using the tools of bonding and boundaries

Rodney and Nancy Dean, M.F.C.C.

Church Growth Institute

Providing Practical Tools for Growth

P.O. Box 4404, Lynchburg, VA 24502

Library of Congress Cataloging-in-Publication Data

Dean, Rodney, 1939–
    Building family values : using the tools of bonding and boundaries
    / Rodney & Nancy Dean.
        p. cm.
    Includes bibliographical references.
    ISBN 0-941005-98-4
    1.   Family--United States--Religious aspects--Christianity.
2.   Parenting--United States--Religious aspects--Christianity.
I.   Dean, Nancy, 1941– . II. Title.
HQ536.D35   1994
306.85--dc20   93-41667
                                                    CIP

Editor: Cindy G. Spear
Editorial & Design Assistant: Tamara Johnson
Cover Designer: Carolyn R. Phelps

Unless otherwise noted, Scripture references are quoted in the King
James Version of the Holy Bible.

Dedicated to

Heather, Jennifer and Chip (Rodney II) who learned family values with us as we bonded and refined boundaries.

Acknowledgments

We thank God for our family where we have and are forbearing with each other in our growing and learning process of relationships. The immeasurable investment our own parents and siblings put into us is reflected in much of our family.

We sincerely thank our instructors who have shared their knowledge and hearts with us.

To the churches we have pastored, we appreciate not only the invaluable extended family life they provided for us, but the genuine contribution the many individuals made to help rear our children by loving them and affirming them.

The leaders in the Minirth-Meier Clinic have had a profound effect on us, both by modeling their commitment to the help and healing of hurting people and by their insights and practical approaches, some of which are included herein.

To the staff and colleagues with whom we love and labor at Canyon Springs Hospital and Canyon Counseling Center, thank you for your inspiration and dedication.

We appreciate our publisher's and editors' commitment to serving people and churches. God bless them in this work.

Finally, we respect and appreciate the many families and individuals that have entrusted and shared their frustrations and pain with us. We owe to them much insight as we journey with them in their growth. We feel honored to be a part of their lives.

CONTENTS

Introduction

INTRODUCTION

Understanding and applying principles of bonding and boundaries is the key in developing and maintaining healthy families. An unhealthy family and its members have difficulty pleasing and being effective for God. When the home is filled with conflict, turmoil and stress, the energy and attention of that family is turned inward, which distracts them from effective service to God in seeking His kingdom first. In fact, the writer to the Hebrews instructs the believer to "throw off everything that hinders and the sin that so easily entangles and let us run with perseverance the race marked out for us" (Heb. 12:1, NIV). If poor family health is a distraction to our service to God, then this injunction is applicable in the context of the family. In order to please God with effective service and the joy of family living as God intended it, we need to learn what things need to be thrown off and how to throw them off.

This book deals with just one segment of healthy families – one large segment.

The main point of this book is that healthy families are those that keep bonding and boundaries in balance.

Healthy Family
Figure I-1

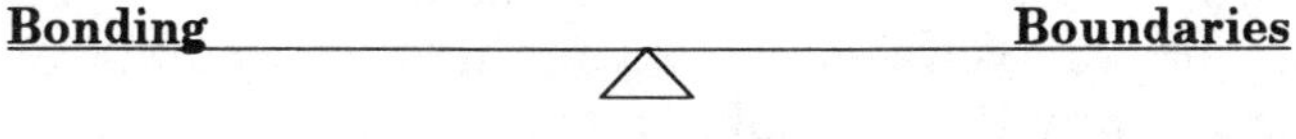

Bonding   **Boundaries**

When a family, or a family member, is out of balance and is too bonded or has too-strict boundaries, it tends toward an unhealthy state. (Illustrated on the following page.)

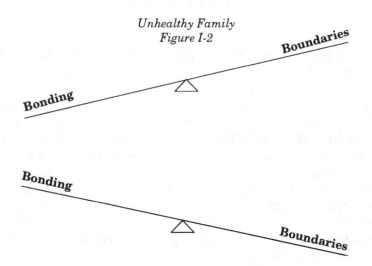

Unhealthy Family
Figure I-2

The purpose of this book is to help families move toward greater health by recognizing where bonding and boundaries need to be adjusted. This assumes that they will be freed up to relate to one another in a more satisfying way as God intended family life to be.

A definition of terms is necessary. Bonding is that emotional strength of cohesiveness that shows itself in feelings of love and joy in a relationship. In bonding, one person feels value and gives value to the other person and desires to be with that person to support, share his or her life, and to protect. There is a specialness and general feeling of gratefulness for the other person. Can you say this is the way you feel about your spouse or children, and is this the way they feel about you?

Bonding brings couples and families together. It makes their relationship one in which the effectiveness of the family as a whole is greater than the summation of the individual effectiveness of each family member.

Two are better than one, because they have a good return for their work: If one falls down, his friend can help him up. But pity the man who falls and has no one to help him up! Also if two lie down together, they will keep warm. But how can one keep warm alone? Though one may be overpowered, two can defend themselves. A cord of three strands is not quickly broken (Eccl. 4:9-12, NIV).

The Ecclesiastes 4 passage sets forth a bonding relationship in which one can help the other up if they fall, keep each other warm when its cold, and defend each other in danger. When this bonding extends to three or more, from married couple to the family, it is even a stronger cord.

This is bonding. It is a relationship that builds mutual emotional strength and is characterized by feelings of love, joy, and gratefulness in the relationship. It makes being together a joy, not a constant tension and conflict and mutual competition. Bonding makes the home a pleasant place to be. Without bonding the home is rigid, cool, and at its best tolerable. Bonding also forms a foundation for a family to please God in interpersonal relationships and frees it for looking to the needs of others.

Bonding is good! Sometimes our mentality is that if it's good, the more there is of it, the better it is. This is not necessarily so. Bonding must be in balance with boundaries.

Boundaries are like invisible fences that surround us and our family, and that regulate the amount of contact that we have with others. They define who we are as well as protect our separateness and autonomy (Nichols and Schwartz, 1991). We are one as a family unit, but each family member is a separate person. Because of who we are, we have different beliefs, values, opinions, and responsibilities. In a Christian family these would basically be anchored in a personal relationship with God and in the teaching of His Word. But even when this is true, there will be many areas of difference. Family members may have different beliefs about the second coming of

Christ or what personality traits they value in a spouse, as well as differing opinions on a variety of topics. They can define themselves as one family but in so doing they do not surrender their personal identity. Each one has boundaries, invisible fences, that protect their identity and enable them to make decisions in life on their own. The family is like the body as described in 1 Corinthians 12:12.

> The body is a unit, though it is made up of many parts; and though all its parts are many, they form one body (NIV).

The body is one but it is made up of different members. As the eye and the ear differ in the human body, so it is in the body of Christ as each member has a different function and identity. As the hand is different from the eye, so the different family members are different from one another with different roles, personalities, and giftedness. Yet they form one family.

If our boundaries as a family or as individuals are too rigid, people cannot get close. If they are too diffuse then people can get too close and control and overinfluence a person so much so that the person loses his or her identity.

These are crucial issues today as far as evaluating the healthy functioning of individuals and families. By God's grace the following chapters will help each family and each family member grow in their spiritual and emotional health. "For God has not given us a spirit of fear; but of power, and of love, and of a sound mind" (2 Tim. 1:7). Love, power, and a sound mind, both in the family unit and in individual family members, glorify God.

Another term, introduced in Chapter 3, is skilling. This term is used to describe the process of developing and using needed skills, especially in the area of self-differentiation. By separating what we feel from what we really need – skilling – we have a better chance of winning and succeeding as a family.

Chapter One

CHAPTER 1
Bonding: The Scent of a Family

The wafting aroma of incense found its way into the early Roman city. "They're victors! They've won!" went up in cheers. The cobblestone road leading into the exuberant city was quickly lined with rejoicing citizens. The much-desired fragrance could now be seen flowing from the lifted urns atop the warrior's lofty poles. Returning from battle, the proud soldiers had been true to their mission, victory, the core of their existence. They had fought hard and kept one focus before them – the pleasing of their homeland and their loved ones. And now they marched in triumph amidst the waving and cheering crowds. How sweet and pleasing was that fragrant aroma of victory. Without telegraphs or any electronic systems, the people depended upon the potpourri of burning incense to precede their warriors home and communicate the assurance of their victory to those who loved them. Its fragrance traditionally communicated triumph and brought joy to its receivers. Fragrances in the air were a symbol of the dedicated warrior's victory and sacrificial offering for their loved ones. You can imagine how much pleasure it brought to those they loved.

The apostle Paul compares us to these dedicated soldiers. People who see a meaning to their lives, a purpose, have a central focus or core from which to continually adjust all behavior. Their purpose in life influences all choices. As you begin your adventure of looking at God's expectations of the family, you need an "unction" – a driving force. This unction applied to the enclosed skillings will produce "a sweet-smelling sacrifice and a fragrant aroma offered to God" (Eph. 5:2, NIV). Victory of love and character in our relationship with God and others is the central purpose of our existence.

Spiritual fervor motivates change and growth in ourselves and then in our relationships. Victory in our individual lives sends to God a sweet-smelling aroma that pleases Him. But even far more reaching is to believe that the *relationships* in our homes have the power to please God. This belief will give us motivation – unction – to continually grow in understanding and improving your home relationships.

Our families and their interrelationships are to be a sweet-smelling fragrance of victory – just as Christ's sacrifice was to the Father. These relationships can please Him or, if they smell not so sweetly ("stinketh"), grieve Him. May this meaning to relationships give us 'unctions' – a word stronger than motivation – to help us grow in *bonding* and *boundaries*.

Research in human behavior indicates that lack of meaningful bonding with other humans results in any or all of the following six serious dysfunctions:

- Addiction, bonding to false substitutes
- Meaninglessness of life
- Phobias and anxieties
- Panic attacks
- Inability to initiate or maintain marital relationships or establish stable career commitments
- Obsessions and compulsions
- Depression and loneliness

None of the above are a sweet smell of victory to our Lord, but a sad symptom of lack of trust in others and thereby lack of bonding.

Bonding

Carol, a 38-year-old Christian, wife and mother, called my office three times for an appointment. Each time she cancelled, out of anxiety. When the emotional pain of phobias and depression became so strong, she was finally able to keep her appointment. She sat, gently tugging at her medium blond hair, that lay poorly kept about her neck. The tugging seemed to help remind her she was there and alive. She certainly wasn't alive emotionally, or even able to express what her problems were. With care, Carol could have presented herself as an attractive woman, with a bright and talented mind. But clearly, self-care had been lacking. Carol was reticent to talk about her relationship with her husband, because he wouldn't like that. He was totally adverse to her seeking help, and his disapproval of her much-delayed choice now fraught her with self-doubt and self-condemnation. She began to cry. With patience, we began to explore her troubled thinking.

Carol, in the midst of her three children (two sons and a daughter) and husband, was emotionally isolated. Her teenage children were struggling with their own unfulfilled needs and communicated little interest in her. Drew, her husband, took a strong patriarchal stand in the family. His job was to keep everyone in order and to make a living. It had been a long time since Carol had felt close to him or valued by him. Drew derived much of his approval from his parents, who lived in the neighborhood. He often went over and watched sports with his father, staying late for supper, while Carol attempted to gather three teenagers out of their own worlds to sit down and eat with her. This usually ended in disappointment as one would jump up to answer a long phone call, while the other two might argue over their sharing clothing and end up in sulking silence. More lately though, Carol hadn't even been able to manage getting the meals on the table. It was just too hard. And life had become overwhelming for her. In her depression, Carol also had not been able to get interested in intimate times with Drew. His reactionary anger only caused him to stay later at his parents' house.

As Carol's emotional isolation continued to spiral down, she had become plagued with new preoccupations. She began to exert much energy in fear. When the phone would ring, she imagined it might be a perpetrator who would trace her voice and come harm her if she answered it. She felt guilty for making the children take all incoming phone calls. But they seemed to handle them all right without her. If anyone even rarely did ask for her, she would go into a panic attack, breathing hard, palms sweating and heart racing. This only added to her self-shame and isolation. She knew this was not the way a victorious Christian should behave, so she concluded God could not love her either. Other unreasonable fears were growing. Her acute self-doubt was now causing her to question herself as a trustworthy person. She, with despair and self-reproach, explained to me she was concerned that her hands may contain germs that might kill her family if she touched them. She was losing touch with reality.

Her emotional detachment from other humans and God left her sadly unbonded. When we talked about these feelings and I asked if she ever felt cherished, she wept in despair. Not only was this her current status, but she had been prepared to fall into it by her first 18 years of growing up. Her parents were divorced; a distant stepfather had tolerated her while her mother put most of her energies into their small children and in trying to avoid a second divorce. There she was in the crowd again, alone. The feelings in her present home were all too familiar, but this time, they seemed to pile on each other.

The end of this story is miraculous. With hard work on her part, Carol began to place trust in me, and talk about her past and present relationships. We grieved her losses of love and nurturing. She did not remain stuck there, but learned the miracle of *trusting* herself, others, and God. She took little risks, like joining a women's support group, then a part-time job. She gained insight as to her behavior and decreased the self-condemnation wherein she was in a position to receive God's love for her and His fellowship. She learned communication skills to talk to Drew about her feelings and needs. She began to practice Ephesians 4:25, to speak the truth in love. She definitely faced some difficult times, with regression, conflict, and discouragement. But Carol's life began to emit a "sweeter fragrance" to our Lord. Her fears quietly vanished like a bad dream. Being a creative woman, Carol finally started her own business, teaching in craft shops where she made many friends. Her appearance improved dramatically, as she had her unstyled hair coiffured into a sharp bob, and her whole presence radiated with beauty. Drew, though a good man, resisted through much of her journey; it was hard to change roles from being the strong "Rescuer." Eventually he could be heard making remarks of admiration about his innovative and attractive wife. Their mutual trust and bonding finally happened. He cherished and valued her as she did him. With this improvement in their intimacy, he was home more to help handle the much-needed training of their unruly teenagers. Bonding with God and other humans had brought about a healing in Carol.

Bonding is essential to our emotional health. It is the first element of the developmental stages of a person's emotional needs (Erikson). It is based on trust and linked with love. We see its importance when Jesus explained, the whole law is contained in love:

1. To love the Lord your God with all your heart, soul, and mind, and

2. To love your neighbor as yourself.

The answers for Carol lay in the simple profoundness of what Jesus had stressed in the law. But she had never experienced love and bonding herself, much less did she then know how to give them out.

Not only do we need to learn to bond; we must learn to express it in our relationship with God and others. We need to nurture two directions in our bonding: a vertical bonding (God & You) and a horizontal bonding (Others & You).

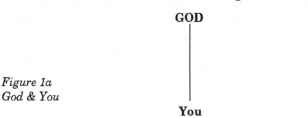

GOD

Figure 1a
God & You

You

Figure 1b
Others & You

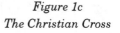

Both directions of bonding are essential in order to be emotionally healthy and happy. Placed together the lines are not only the symbol of our Christian faith, but a reminder of the fulfillment of the whole law.

Figure 1c
The Christian Cross

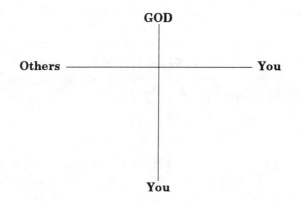

Ephesians 5:2 tells us to "walk in love just as Christ loved you." The introduction spelled out the meaning of bonding. We reiterate here that to feel bonded is to feel loved – significant, valued, cherished. A person who does not experience these feelings will have emotional pain. The implication here is that not only do others need to express worth and love to us, but we have to be able to "metabolize" it – to allow it to come in and be a part of our bones and marrow. Proverbs 16:24, "Pleasant words are as an honeycomb, sweet to the soul, and health to the bones."

Three Models of Bonding Relationships

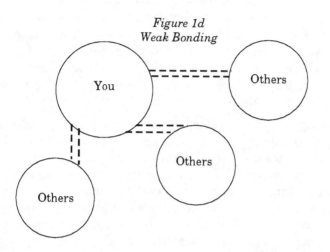

Figure 1d
Weak Bonding

Weak bonding depicts little attachment with others. You might be in a large family or isolated; but emotionally you feel alone in your delights and woes. This is not the model Christ gave us, for living a life of love (Eph. 5:1), both in giving and receiving. Additionally, many emotional symptoms mentioned earlier begin to operate in our lives when we live emotionally isolated. Too many emotional boundaries cut us off from sharing with people.

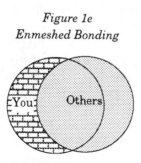

Figure 1e
Enmeshed Bonding

Enmeshed bonding is the opposite of weak bonding, but it can be just as destructive. One person loses himself (or herself) in the other. This is often because of strong control desires in one person. This individual will seek

out someone who unconsciously wants to hide in the identity of another. The hider may allow the other to think,
decide, and dictate how he or she should feel. The hider
has abandoned his/her self and true identity, just like he
or she was abandoned as a child. The hider repeats the
childhood trauma of not being a valued, important person. This is too much bonding, not balanced by the boundaries of identity lines.

Having identical twins, we very consciously encouraged their bonding, but we were also very alert to monitor
any enmeshment in their relationship. In the seventh
month of pregnancy, X-rays clearly revealed Heather's
hand on Jennifer's wrist in the womb. Bonding appeared
to be beginning. Later, when they were about 18 months,
Jennifer was sitting on the couch crying, wanting some
unexplainable request. Heather toddled over, gently
placed Jennifer's thumb in her mouth and wrapped her
favorite "blankey" (blanket) all around her. Now these
two were strongly bonded.

They still are "best friends," Heather was maid of
honor in Jennifer's wedding and Jennifer will be maid of
honor in Heather's wedding, and they care deeply for each
other. Yet, it has been important for them to maintain
their separate identity. They have sought separate circles
of friends, interests, and space. To support this, we put
high priority on their having their own rooms. Many
times, we would have just a "Jennifer Day" and later a
"Heather Day" and always two birthday cakes on their
shared birthday. They have beautifully worked out a very
delicate balance of bonding and boundaries in the complicated relationship of identical twins. They exemplify
the third model.

Figure 1f
Strong, Healthy Bonding

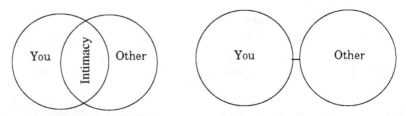

People in strong, healthy bonding relationships love, care, rejoice, and weep with the other, yet maintain their own responsibilities and boundaries. There is a flexibility about these relationships, sometimes moving closer, and sometimes being allowed the space and distance. Their relationship is enjoyable and contributing, rather than smothering or lonely.

Two channels need to be open, the expresser and the receiver. Many people cannot bond because they cannot receive love, though extended to them from many angles. This again is based on trust – taking the risk to be as a child and receive the love given to us by humans, though imperfect and not always consistent. When we have been wounded during our early years of attempting to bond with our caretakers (mom and dad), our trust is damaged. This makes it scary or difficult to trust later and so bond with others. We may strongly resist the vulnerable, open position of childlikeness which is necessary for close bonding. This is our propensity if we were rejected and wounded as a young dependent child.

The good news is that as adults, husbands, wives, and parents we can *learn* to trust and bond. We can do this by monitoring or calling ourselves on our mistrust of one another, and stretching ourselves to take small risks of trust. For example, we need to tell our honest feelings, good and bad. When we withhold what we feel in relationships, we block intimacy. We need to express love and affirmation to those we care about. This is very hard for some. These were some of the specific steps Carol had to practice for her healing and victory. Taking risks toward developing bonding skills is an area to explore with a family therapist if bonding, as you now discover it, is difficult for you to give or receive.

Bonding components are well described by Gary Smalley and John Trent in their book, *The Blessing*. While they do not use the term "bonding," they describe building a blessing into each individual life within the family – much like the valued blessing the Old Testament fathers gave to their children. Building this blessing in the family also results in building the essential bonding between family members. Some of these components are:

- A meaningful touch
- A spoken message (of gratefulness)
- Attaching "high value" to the one being blessed (*The Blessing*, p. 24)

Carol had not received these interactions in either of her families. The meaningful touch has been a verified need backed by numerous studies. Even baby monkeys have maintained survival by obtaining their needed milk from the set-up, cold-wire mother monkey while clinging tenaciously with their other hand to the soft terry cloth mother without a bottle. They needed the tender feel of softness for their emotional and physical survival. We all need a tender touch, a physical human connection that says you are valued, loved. A child builds his self-image by the way he is handled. If he is jerked around, slapped about, it follows that he sees himself as a less than worthy item, much like a rag.

I walked out of my office last week to observe a small 2-year-old boy, feeling very proud of himself as he made the momentous effort to step down from the curb of the parking lot. I watched his gleeful face as he balanced on one foot and was enjoying his personal conquest of balance. Just as he was attempting another brave, balancing maneuver, his little face changed immediately from glee to hurt, and then squalling anger. His father now ready to leave the area, had come from behind, grabbed his arm, abruptly jerking him around the other direction with the statement: "Come on, we've got to go now!" He left, half lifting the screaming toddler off the ground and suspending him by one arm. What the little person had accomplished and was feeling, was clearly not valued by a significant person in his life, his father. How could he argue with himself that his accomplishments or feelings were important? If this is a continual pattern of their relationship, this little person is a candidate for low self-esteem, mistrust, and lack of parental bonding.

In contrast, children whose feelings and values or efforts are esteemed will be prepared for considering themselves the valuable person they are. If you did not receive the meaningful touch, gentle affirming physical interactions, you may need to risk trying and practicing them in order to build healthy relationships with the members of your family.

Within the family, a touch on the shoulder, a stroke of the hair, an affirming hug and affectionate kiss communicate you are valued.

Two other common withdrawals of the meaningful touch center around fathers and sons, and parents with opposite sex adolescents. Following our twin daughters and the advent of our son, I vividly recall Rod innocently asking, "Do fathers kiss their little boys?" We now laugh at that early concern, for once that precious blond-haired, blue-eyed little fellow lived among us, the earlier myth that fathers don't kiss boys was abandoned. Commonly, Chip may receive a playful headlock, while Dad threatens to kiss his ears off. Yes, sons need affection from their fathers to give them the message of self-worth.

In my office, many women repeatedly relate their feelings of abandonment to about the age of 13. They seem puzzled as to what was occurring, but feel personal devaluation by the physical rejection. Due to no plan of their own, they were becoming young women. Their fathers took this as a cue to pull away from the meaningful touch, often because of fear of their own sexuality. This may have been happening in Carol's first home, with her stepfather ignoring her. Confusion and low self-value are left in the mind of the growing adolescent. The father needs to have a godly attitude toward his sexuality, and, if married, be strongly bonded to his wife, physically and emotionally. If single, he needs to be bonded in other godly and healthy relationships. The father is then free to give the kindly, fatherly affection the daughter so clearly deserves. Obviously her young womanhood needs to be respected, and the affection is less intimate, but the father or stepfather must always communicate value and love. Conversely, mother and son relationships require the meaningful touch with love and discretion. I may not caress and hold my teenage son as I did when he was a tiny boy, but he surely gets his share of back scratches and hardy hugs, giving him one straight message: you are loved and valued. The following section describes practical scenes of the meaningful touch and the spoken word in families.

The Cycle of Bonding: Trust ♦ Gratefulness ♦ Self-Esteem ♦ Bonding ♦ Trust

Trust for each others' best interest, within the family members, is at the root of bonding. It is the first and basic emotional need for each of us, which began when we were newborns. It continues to be at the root of all relationships.

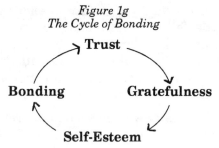

Figure 1g
The Cycle of Bonding

The cycle of bonding begins with trust and ultimately culminates around again to build our trust in God. Moving through this cycle allows us to be able to obey Him and bond with Him – to be that "sweet smelling sacrifice" to Him. Trust must be built in a family by keeping our word, speaking the truth, being who we say we are, and being predictable to one another – knowing the inner self of one another. Mind alterers, such as alcohol and drugs as well as any addictions, sabotage trust in a family.

Only by feelings of trust and *gratefulness* for one another within the family, would each one want to give the blessing to one another. This heartfelt appreciation for each other is crucial in order to make the efforts and the commitment to maintain life-giving bonding. "What you sow, you also reap."

When our son Chip was about 8, as was our custom, I was putting him to bed with talk and prayers. I was stroking his hair and telling him of some things I liked about him and how thankful I was he was our son (gratefulness), when he responded with a memorable bonding moment. He piped in and said, "Why Mom, when I was up in heaven before I was born, I had to fight off all the other babies to get to come live with you and Dad." Now that may not be theologically correct, but it sure made me feel appreciated and loved in his little blue eyes – and it felt good – to both of us! Gratefulness nurtured bonding.

Unresolved anger, resentment, vindictiveness, and personal low self-esteem are monsters that deteriorate a spirit of gratefulness for others. Possessing a negative attitude is the opposite of gratefulness. "You never keep your word." "I probably won't see what you borrowed ever again." "What's the use of trying to have fun with this family?" A negative attitude is the result of early trust wounds. This negative spirit perpetuates a second generation of unmet emotional needs in the children. Thus, there is a prevailing attitude of ungratefulness in the family. Again, learning to look for the good things others are and do, pointing them out, and commenting with "kindness words" demonstrates your appreciation toward each other. These are practical moves toward changing a negative attitude to a grateful attitude, which in turn increases trust, which increases bonding.

With all the years of education and degrees Rod has obtained, I believe one of the most profound, effective statements he makes as a father to our son is, "What a guy! Mom, isn't he some guy?" as he fondly smiles and taps him on the shoulder. Rod, 17 years old, needs appreciation for just being himself. Other phrases that bespeak gratefulness and need to ring in the walls of our homes are:

"We've sure got a champ!" "Good morning, Princess." "I'm so thankful for you." "How's my wonderful husband?" A favorite of mine from my husband is, "You're all I need!"

Unaffirming communication begets low self-esteem. Negative statements such as, "What's the matter with you?" "Can't you ever do anything right?" "You're a mess!" "Why can't you be like Joey across the street?" engender self-protection statements like, "It's not my fault!" "Shut up!" "Get off my back!" These communications stem from lack of trust increasing the ungratefulness to each other. This results in low self-esteem for the recipients of the verbal abuse. Clearly, their bonding is blocked which repeats the cycle of lack of trust.

Figure 1h
The Cycle of Mistrust

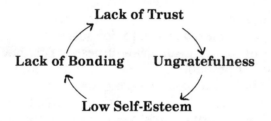

Fortunately, as we have seen, the cycle can be virtuous as well as vicious: honest communication engenders high self-esteem which encourages more bonding and around we go the other way (Satire, 1972, 1988).

Low self-esteem, because of its inherent self-protective tendencies, blocks and actually prevents intimate bonding. While high self-esteem, with its inherently trusting and grateful tendencies, builds bonding within its family members. Because of the trust inherent in people with high self-esteem, they can speak honestly what they are feeling and experiencing. This honest communication is especially important regarding the emotional impact they have on each other within the family, and regarding family communication rules. (Mutual respect, family communication rules are covered later).

Someone has said that it takes six positive statements to our children for every one negative statement to balance them out in order to maintain good self-esteem. As a mother I find this a challenging rule to observe, particularly in the face of seeing the need to correct children about table manners and tennis shoes left in the middle of the den floor, etc. Occasionally, Rod hears me listing off my constructive negativisms. I feel a little touch on my shoulder, with a friendly reminder, "Remember the six to one rule." Sometimes it takes conscious effort to sandwich in the honest appreciation comments with the necessary directions.

Norm Wakefield talks about three dimensions of self-esteem:

- Belonging – having a sense of security and identity with others who love, accept, and support me.

- Worth – being affirmed as a person of value, being cherished and respected.

- Competence – gaining a sense of achievement, being affirmed as an able person.

Each of these dimensions are clearly important components of a person's self-esteem. Evidence indicates that the dimensions are obtained by what we hear about ourselves and what we say to each other. These messages result in a person feeling like they belong, like they have worth, and like they have competence. Our belonging, worth, and competence are obtained by how we talk to each other in the family. Again, our communication is motivated or blocked by whether or not we have a spirit of gratefulness for each other. Trust, gratefulness, and high self-esteem all lead to bonding within a family. This all leads back into trusting each other, increasing the gratefulness, building high self-esteem, then back to a bonded family. And so it goes around and around in a very positive joyful circle. The more the cycle goes around in thousands of daily incidents and communications, the more the family is bonded.

As family members, we need to be stress relievers to each other, not stressors to each other. And while the latter is unavoidable at times, we need to monitor our talk and deeds, sincerely attempting to build each other up and walk in love (Eph. 5:1).

What Bonding Looks Like and Experientially Feels Like:

- A young girl finds love and acceptance from a mother who eagerly awaits her arrival home from school.

- A young mother celebrates the joy of greeting her son and daughters as she was greeted by her grateful mother.

- A wife feels affirmed and cherished from the enthusiastic greetings of her husband.

These are the colors and shapes of bonding, to one who questions its exact appearance. Throughout a lifetime, bonding displays many faces and plays a crucial role in developing an individual's self-esteem.

When I was a young girl, I would come home from school, my arms usually loaded with books. The scene I recall stands out strong in my memories. My mother at that time was a homemaker; and she usually wore an apron. I can still see her in my mind's eye, so very clearly, coming from the kitchen, through the dining room, her body posture leaned forward a bit, usually drying her hands on her apron. Her eyes bright, she had a happiness about her face and an eagerness in her step as she was coming to greet me. I wouldn't get very far from the door before I would feel both of her arms around me, and despite the load of books in my arms and what not, she would swing me around, enthusiastically proclaiming, "How's the most wonderful girl that ever lived? How's the most beautiful girl on two legs? My Nancy!"

Because I can so clearly remember this, it obviously had a positive effect on me. This is what bonding looks and feels like. I truly felt significant, even if I knew I wasn't the most beautiful girl that ever walked or even the most wonderful girl, I certainly felt significant in my

Mom's eyes. I felt like I was missed after being gone at school all day and I felt valued. From there, Mom would usually lead me into the kitchen where a tasty snack awaited me. In a time where mothers work and schedules are perhaps accelerated, each of these events may not be feasible, but some way we need to take the time to greet those who we've been separated from, to let them know that they're important to us and that we're glad to see them again.

When I have shared that scene in the psychiatric clinic where I teach, tears often appear in various individual's eyes as they see where they did not have bonding, where they did not feel valued or significant or wonderful in the eyes of their family. If you did not experience strong bonding in your family of origin, you can watch families who have it, read books about it, take risks to try it, and you can learn it. You can start a new series of generations that passes down strong bonding to the glory of God.

Because of what was handed to me, I really enjoy greeting my kids when they come home. They too get the repeated swinging in the arms and accolades of being the "most wonderful son or daughter in the world." In fact, when my husband and I greet, we generally find each other upon arriving home, clasp our arms around each other, and jump up and down. This is a tradition which began when we first got married and were so glad to see each other when we first got home. As the years go by, some of our jumps are a little slow and tired, but they still say, "You're worth the greeting. I'm really glad to see you."

When Rod and I were first married, he was in graduate Bible school and I was a young school teacher. He would arrive home to our little rented brick bungalow, nestled in 14 towering pine trees in the heart of South Carolina. I vividly remember the afternoons of driving up in front of the cozy little place, feeling tired from 30 little third-graders. As I looked through the pines into the large picture window of the home, my energy would renew; and I could not restrain a huge smile across my face. There, with drapes wide open, was Rod – the man with ever-mature deportment in public and the lieutenant-commander, navel-officer that he was – jumping up and down and turning in circles, expressing his glee that I had come home. Bonding was strong, refreshing to the body and spirit, and easy then for me to reciprocate. The little walk through the pines to the front door would take but seconds, when we could jump up and down together. Thus, our tradition continues some 27 years later, with only a few modifications.

As a family therapist, I often hear, "she won't even quit washing the dishes" or "she's always on the phone when I come home." Message: "I'm insignificant." Or "He just keeps on reading his paper when I come in" or "I can't unglue him from the T.V. news to talk about our day." Message: "I'm uncherished." It is safe to say that greeting and parting with love are two important faces in bonding.

Bonding gives the feeling that "I'm on your team and I want to help you get what you need." Bonding can be seen in a mother helping her daughter be as pretty as she possibly can and caring about her concerns. Bonding is caring about the son's desire for doing well in athletics and helping him with protein drinks or whatever he thinks will help build his strength. Bonding sounds like listening as a father and son express their feelings to one another. Bonding has a lot of everyday practical faces and sounds.

Summary

We have the capability of pleasing God by the quality of our relationships in the family. These relationships have the power to be the sacrifice of a "sweet smelling fragrance to our God" or a stench to His nostrils. We truly have such "a great cloud of witnessess" (Heb. 11:1). The burning unction of a Christian needs to be: to grow in a loving bond, both vertically with Jesus Christ and horizontally with significant people around us (Gen. 2:18, 1 John 4:21). The family unit needs to be committed to bonding with a balance of boundaries, and therefore understand what bonding is and what it looks like.

Learning to Trust*

There's a father in your sweetest dreams
Who's always there to meet your needs
He never ever lets you down
There's a mother in your heart of hearts
Who always plays the perfect part

She never lets you hit the ground
This is the need of children
These are their tender dreams
And on how it hurts when they don't come true

Chorus

(That's why I'm) Learning to trust in you
In everything I do
Learning to trust in you
'Cause I know in my heart that you're true
I'm learning to trust in you
But sometimes it's so hard to do

Father, little children must grow up
And to grow up we've got to learn to trust
And to trust we've got to cling to you
And when you tell me you will hold me close
It's the very hardest thing I do

I've got this pain inside me
It speaks to me loud and clear;
When there's so much to gain
there's always so much to lose

Keep calling me calling me closer
Don't let me hold back
Whatever it takes I must break through
The heart of the child is broken
But his time has come
Whatever he lost I'll find in you.

*Words by Michael Hudson and David Meece; music by David Meece.
© 1989 by Meece Music (admin. by Word, Inc.) and Ariose Music (admin. by Gaither Copyright Management). Used by permission.

Reflective Questions

1. What is the ultimate purpose of your family? Can you state it in ten words or less?

2. Do you feel bonded to your family? What feelings does that bring up for you?

3. Can you reflect on scenes of when you felt bonded as a child or perhaps of how you would like to have felt bonded – valued, connected, loved?

Discussion Questions

1. What are some ways to increase the quality of bonding in a family?

2. How can the crucial components of bonding increasingly be expressed in your family?

    a. Trust

    b. Gratefulness

    c. Self-Esteem

3. List some opportune moments for giving the meaningful touch and the spoken word to communicate value to one another – beginning with the husband and wife, then to the children.

Chapter Two

CHAPTER 2
Boundaries: The Identity of Family Members

What then is the balance of Bonding, but Boundaries?
These are modern-day terms to help us visualize and act
out successful relationships, especially in the family.
What are boundaries in a family? Boundaries are unseen
property lines of each family member, keeping them from
being one enmeshed mass, where one hides in the identity
of the other or dominates another's growth or autonomy.
Boundaries are a sense of ourselves; they help us see how
we are different from others – physically, intellectually,
and emotionally. They are symbolic fences which have
three purposes:

- to keep people from coming into our space and
  abusing us

- to keep us from going into the space of others and
  abusing them

- to give each of us a way to embody our sense of
  "who we are" (Mellody, p. 11, 1987)

Are Boundaries Godly?

Paul addressed this concept with sarcasm to the Corinthians.

> For you, being so wise, bear with the foolish glad-
> ly. For you bear with anyone if he enslaves you, if
> he devours you, if he takes advantage of you, if he
> exalts himself, if he hits you in the face. To my
> shame I must say that we have been weak by
> comparison. But in whatever respect anyone else
> is bold (I speak in foolishness), I am just as bold
> myself (2 Cor. 11:19-21).

Paul suggests that the Corinthians were not strong
enough to say "no" to enslaving, devouring people; but
that he did know how to be bold enough to withstand

them crossing his boundaries. Clearly, Paul's life exemplified a man of clear beliefs, values, opinions, and responsibilities. Through grace, his strong faith, and these well-defined boundaries, Paul was mightily used of God. He, with the many other earthshaking apostles, such as James, was not "...like a wave of the sea driven with the wind and tossed...being a double-minded man is unstable in all his ways" (James 1:6, 8).

Jesus was the perfect example of a well-boundaried person. He knew and maintained His mission, not letting Satan distract Him into considering Satan's value system, that of ruling the kingdoms of the world with all their glory (Matt. 4:8-9). Yet Jesus loved and interacted with people in such a compassionate and flexible manner, considering their feelings and needs. He looked at people with compassion and saw them as weary and scattered sheep without a shepherd (Matt. 9:36). His boundaries were balanced with His bonding. He heard the needs of His wedding host, and performed His first miracle by turning their water into wine (John 2:3-9) – hardly a rigid, isolated overly-boundaried mentality. At the same time, Jesus explains that He came to set a sword among families (Matt. 10:34-38, NIV).

> Do not think that I came to bring peace on the earth; I did not come to bring peace on the earth; I did not come to bring peace, but a sword. For I came to set a man against his father, and daughter against her mother, and a daughter-in-law against her mother-in-law; and a man's enemies will be the members of his household. He who loves father or mother more than Me is not worthy of Me; and he who loves son or daughter more than Me is not worthy of Me. And he who does not take his cross and follow after Me is not worthy of Me.

Where it would be necessary, even family members would have to stand for their individual beliefs and values at the cost of conflict or separation – maintaining their boundaries around their inner convictions.

"Boundaried people are the least angry people in the world."

– Dr. John Townsend

Jesus' often-quoted teaching of "turn the other cheek" in Matthew 5:39 may cause someone to consider boundaries as ungodly. Jesus' topic was not the laying aside of personal boundaries. Rather it was the principle of replacing the Old Testament law of retaliation, "an eye for an eye and a tooth for a tooth" (Matt. 5:38), with a new law of enduring hardships and not resorting to revenge. He taught the people, with a hyperbole (exaggeration), to illustrate the new law of His kingdom – love.

Healthy-boundaried people will not need to be driven by anger and revenge. Instead they will recognize their responsibilities within their property lines and take steps to stop personal abuse, without needing to punish the abuser. Someone without healthy boundaries may believe they deserve the abuse or they may be consumed with revenge or effort to control behavior within another person's property lines.

Jesus' response to the Pharisees in Matthew indicates His clear ability and practice of verbalizing boundaries. When they had been testing Him, disrespecting His identity, and attempting to trap Him (Matt. 22:15), He did not allow their underlying motives to control his emotions and actions. He saw their intentions and rebuked them sternly for it. "Why are you testing me, you hypocrites" (Matt. 22:18)? He continued by answering their question, but without revenge. He directly told them how He felt and what they were doing that was false. He set boundaries of what He would allow to penetrate into His personal emotional space. He clearly did not store up anger nor was He controlled by resentment because of their behavior. He instead stated His beliefs, His values, His opinions, and His responsibilities to reveal truth and maintain His identity. What a model for us in our everyday relationships of how to apply boundaries!

How Can We Become Boundaried People?

When we decide what we believe are our values and responsibilities, we gain a sense of who we are – so vital to self-esteem and mental health.

More specifically, this sense of self or identity is the:

- Beliefs of an individual member

- Values of an individual member

- Opinions and feelings of an individual member

- Responsibilities of an individual member

　(Dr. John Townsend, Director of Minirth/Meier Clinic West)

I have coined the word **BVORs** (pronounced bavors), your beliefs, values, opinions, and responsibilities, because we will regularly refer to these as crucial aspects of what is in your boundaries. Without developed BVORS within a person's property lines, the walls of the boundaries will collapse and fall into an empty space within the person. The put-down term "air-head" describes the extreme of a person with such an empty space within them. Their boundaries continually fall down into that space because they have not developed their BVORs, and do not know who they are. All of us are at different levels of developed BVORs. A person optimally develops his or her BVORs between 13 and 21 years old (Erikson's Psycho-Social Developmental Stages). This, then, prepares him/her for the next developmental task, that of career choice and mate selection.

Considering that none of us came from perfectly modeled environments, most of us are yet working on this development of who we are. Kohlberg, a renowned social scientist, is famous for his research on the moral development of humans. He concludes that over 50 percent of adults have not reached above 13 years old in their moral development. Most people remain in the child (10-13 years) role of being motivated in their choices by the desire to avoid disapproval or dislike of others. The mature adult orientation would be to have the strength to know, in your own conscience, what is moral, and then abide by it. People need to develop their BVORs, then have boundaries to maintain them.

We will cover more of *what* is in your boundaries, your BVORs, which will be necessary to understand in order to develop well-defined boundaries. First we need to describe the path there, the *"how to's"* to build BVORs. In the field of psychology, we use a term called "centering." Centering is essential for decreasing a frenetic, empty, lifestyle that is based on not knowing who you are as a person. This is very significant for the Christian. We must center; spend daily time before God and in His Word in order to know what we truly and deeply believe. Our beliefs are established on what we have faith in. Our faith comes by hearing, and hearing by the Word of God (Rom. 10:17). Deep convictions from our beliefs lead us to action, energy, change – changing us more into His likeness. The exciting fact about growing in bonding and boundaries, is that it is learned behavior. The legacy from our family of origin about how we bonded and did or did not have boundaries was only learned from them. Now we have the adult responsibility to choose what we want to keep from that legacy and what we choose to learn for ourselves. This learning to love and to take individual responsibility for our beliefs and lives must have God's truth and power working daily in us. "Belief is the result of consideration, doubt, reasoning, and concluding. The ability to form beliefs is the mark of God's image in our life" (*The Life Recovery Bible*, notes p. 1229). God amazingly made us like Himself, able to form beliefs and values.

> So God created man in his own image, in the image of God created he him; and female created he them (Gen. 1:27).

God made us like Himself with the ability to think, relate to Him, and conclude clear, solid beliefs, values, opinions/feelings, and responsibilities like He does.

The practicalities of setting the alarm clock at least 20 to 30 minutes earlier or structuring a time in the evening to center yourself with your Creator and in His Word is essential, not only to build strong BVORs, but to maintain them in a society that continually gives ungodly messages, ungodly BVORs, to us. Family devotions are also vital if we are to effectively pass down our BVORs to our children.

I like to learn as much as I can about heartache vicariously, from other's experiences, because I don't have any desire to go through any more than absolutely necessary. A dear Christian friend of ours shocked us by leaving his wife and children for an affair. After much tragedy and sorrow, he repented and returned to his family. Since we had been close friends, I took the opportunity to ask him an important question: What could he tell me about what had caused such a catastrophe, so that our family, being only of like flesh, could avoid such a pitfall? I will always remember his answer. "I quit looking at Jesus...I started taking my Bible to my office to have my devotions there to save time; only there, the phone rang, and people wanted me, to where I soon just wasn't looking at Him." This really struck me. I believe our strength lies in knowing our weakness. We're all of weak flesh, capable of anything, if in the right circumstances and without the power of Christ. This is truly verified, as every week in my office, well-meaning – even Christian people – cry or are angered over the addiction of an affair. While this is only one ploy of Satan to make our family relationships a "stench that reaches to heaven" (Gen. 1:13), our hope for building the beliefs and values wherein He created us to be like Him, lies in meeting regularly with Him and in His Word. I continue to include His Word, because I observe many Christians say, "I pray every day," but it is often only a grocery list of their wants, not the cutting away and healing work of the Word of God.

> The word of God is living and active and sharper than any two-edged sword, and piercing as far as the division of soul and spirit, of both joints and

marrow, and able to judge the thought and intentions of the heart (Heb. 4:12).

Praise God for the miracles His spirit can do in us through His Word, and that He has made us to learn and to grow with each generation! If you don't have a plan for consistent daily devotions, consider the *Life Recovery Bible*. It is loaded with daily plans for encountering God, including a 12 step-plan.

When our daughter, Heather, was about 16, she and I were out having a bite to eat together. As I asked her how things were going at high school, she began to explain to me of the frustration she was feeling toward one of her friends. It seemed that when her peer, Anna, was with her, she was clean-cut, fun, upright and fit in with Heather's moral system. However, Heather complained, "I don't know what is the matter with her. I go to school the next Monday, and hear how Anna got drunk with some other friends over the weekend." Since this seemed a pattern with her, I replied to Heather, "Anna's problem is she doesn't know *who she is*." Truly, her BVORs were not developed and she displayed very weak boundaries. These only tumbled in under pressure, causing her to be "double-minded and unstable in all her ways" (James 1:8). I believe the difference was, Heather knew more of who she was – what her BVORs were, and thus maintained stronger boundaries.

The "what" of our BVORs are, indeed, our identity.

The BVORs of a person can be considered from both a broad perspective as well as an everyday, more detailed view. Broadly speaking, your *beliefs* cover topics like, who you think God is, what you believe is the purpose of living, moral decisions, political and social ideas, your role in the family scheme, and so forth. Many times we don't really have beliefs about very important issues of life and therefore join in on whatever those around us are doing. Or we have very low energy or motivation in life to act upon an issue, because our belief is not developed or it is riddled with doubt (James 1:3).

The development of your *values* gives unction for what is keenly important to you – what you really love. Values are the hierarchy or priority of your beliefs. We can identify them by where we put our energy, time, and finances. Broad areas of values would be the importance we place on worshipping and serving God, building family relationships, our physical and mental health, friendships, loyalties to our country, importance of financial security, etc.

Your *opinions and feelings* stem from the core of what is going on inside of you – your ideas; your thinking; even your feelings of love, joy, peace or anger, and depression or anxiety. If we suppress or are unaware of what opinions and feelings are stirring around inside us, we again have little zest for life and truly don't know ourselves. If I don't know myself, how can I share myself with you (bonding)? Or how can I individuate myself from you (boundaries)? Not knowing what we are thinking or what we are feeling is called "being out of touch with our feelings." This often causes us to react with an inappropriate feeling. For example: A man is really feeling sad that he broke his saw, but since he is out of touch with what he is really feeling, he may copy a behavior he has witnessed, like throwing the broken saw across the room in anger. In actuality, his opinion is that he really liked that saw and realized a loss, and, therefore, felt sad to have broken it. Because he cannot touch or discern his actual feelings, he is influenced by others' behavior (at rage) and opinion (that "macho" men react that way) and has little self-control.

Your *responsibilities* are a major outworking of your identity. From a broader perspective, your responsibilities include personal commitment to the areas of: Financial, Intellectual, Social, Spiritual, Emotional, and Physical commitments. These are not necessarily in order, but make up the F.I.S.S.E.P. Wheel. If any of the spokes are missing or weak, one's ride on the road of life is going to be bumpy and uncomfortable.

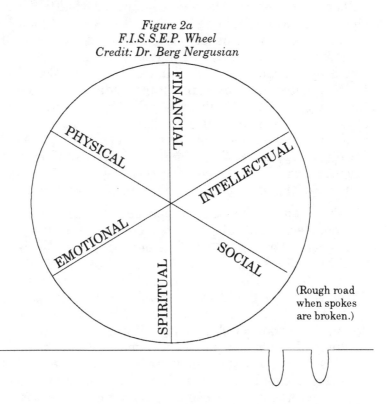

Figure 2a
F.I.S.S.E.P. Wheel
Credit: Dr. Berg Nergusian

(Rough road when spokes are broken.)

When I am not conscientiously committed to developing these areas of personal responsibility, I let my boundaries fall down, and other people may take over my responsibilities. This results in my feeling depressed, anxious or even angry. For instance, if I am not developing and taking care of my financial obligations, others often criticize or tell me what to do, or even take over my money.

Sometimes, like when we were kids, we would rather wash the neighbor's dishes than our own. We would perhaps, neglect our own spiritual development (F.I.S.S.E.P. spoke), while we worry about telling others how to do theirs. This is not to say we should not share or care about each other, but not at the expense of our own development. To watch your own obligations of personal health, emotional well-being, etc., is not narcissistic but rather it is responsible and boundaried (Matt. 7 principle). It is even humbling to admit that if I don' t do this, I will have symptoms of being unboundaried, i.e., depression, anger or anxiety. I may not, then, be the sweet-smelling fragrance to God that He desires (2 Cor. 2:15). Each member of the family must individually develop these components of their personality to be a mature, autonomous person. Yet, most adults probably have not successfully internalized this personal identity process. In 1 Corinthians 12:14-21 Paul sounds very similar as he discusses the importance of respecting each individual member of the body of Christ, with his or her unique gifts:

> For even as the body is one and yet has many members, and all the members of the body, though they are many, are one body, so also is Christ. For by one Spirit we were all baptized into one body, whether Jews or Greeks, whether slaves or free, and we were all made to drink of one Spirit. For the body is not one member, but many. If the foot should say, "Because I am not a hand, I am not a part of the body," it is not for this reason any the less a part of the body. And if the ear should say, "Because I am not an eye, I am not a part of the body," it is not for this reason any the less a part of the body. If the whole body were an eye, where would the hearing be? If the whole were hearing, where would the sense of smell be? But now God has placed the members, each one of them, in the body, just as He desired. And if they were all one member, where would the body be? But now there are many members, but one body. And the eye cannot say to the hand, "I have no need of you;" or again the head to the feet, "I have no need of you" (NIV).

Paul was respecting the boundaries of each person, rather than insisting on their being all the same – cookie cutters. In parallel, each member of the family needs to be committed to respecting the boundaries of each other, with our individual roles and gifts.

Boundaries in a Family

We have refered to being a family with children. For the purpose of "walking in the light" (being vulnerable) so that "we can have fellowship" with you the readers (a type of bonding, 1 John 1:7) and more honestly convey the reality of family bonding and boundaries; we introduce our family. In this introduction of the people we know the best and have lived with, we may insert their inside identity – their beliefs, values, opinions, feelings, and responsibilities – with the hope that alive, struggling, interacting people may reveal this concept more clearly. You will see overlap in the BVORs, but again, our hope is to reveal the essence of what holds up our boundaries, our identities.

We risk the vulnerability of openness to describe our family members because, while admittedly growth is yet in process, the basis of our spiritual and emotional health is bonding and boundaries. They appear to be major and crucial ingredients for much of the joy and goals achieved. The word "risk" was used because we do not wish to sound like we have arrived – far from it; nor do we want anyone to feel discouraged as they endeavor to improve their difficult family relationships. We simply want to be open about sharing what has worked in order to be an encouragement to one another. Family life is not easy for us either; we cry, get mad, struggle at times and we still work on bonding and boundaries.

Rod, 53, is head of our home, husband of 27 years, first marriage, and father of three. He became a Christian at 19 while an engineering student at Colorado State University (his beliefs). He enthusiastically led many fellow students to Christ. He served as an officer in the Naval Air as a Lieutenant Commander for eleven years. Rod has pastored four churches over the past 25 years, including pioneering a new work and being the senior pastor of three other multistaffed larger churches (his values). He now counsels families and studies at Azusa Pacific University Graduate School to complete his Marriage, Family and Child Therapy License (opinion for higher education). He holds a doctorate from Fuller Theological Seminary and never thought he'd return to school at this stage of life (responsibilities). Rod is greatly loved and esteemed by his wife and children – no trite statement (opinion/ feelings). He has a fun personality and has provided thousands of laughing moments to the delight of the Dean clan (values/humor). Rod especially enjoys biking, running and table talks with his family (his values and opinions). He has a consistent deep commitment and bonding to his Savior and then to his wife and children (beliefs). An immeasurably important feeling in his wife and children is that they as a family are second only to God, and that the church and work come after our relationships (values).

Nancy, 52, is wife of 27 years, first marriage, mother of three. Nancy bonded with Christ at a early age of 12. She developed a missionary spirit as a child, sharing with her little friends about Jesus. In high school, she continued her vision for the lost and, with a friend, started a Youth for Christ Club, then initiated an Inter-Varsity Chapter in college (beliefs). Before the children were born and after they were in school, She taught as a learning-disability specialist (part-time) for 20 years. Then, because of a desire to more effectively help families bring honor to Christ, she studied and became licensed as a Marriage, Family and Child Therapist, holding two masters degrees (values/helping others). She now serves families in a thriving private practice as well as setting up and directing the Canyon Christian Treatment Center in a psychiatric hospital. She formerly codirected a Minirth-Meier Clinic (responsibilities). Nancy is creative, loves music, plays the piano, has directed and produced many extensive pageants and musicals in the church. She is known for her positive "up spirit" (her opinions and feelings about beauty and life). She walks in a close bonding with Jesus and is enthusiastic about being a wife and mother (values).

Heather, 23, is single, and a beauty with long, full hair, bright eyes, and a warm smile. While petite of stature, she gained "best girl athlete" in high school as well as saluditorian and student-body president (values putting much into life). Her reputation of being a steadfast, bonded Christian preceded her into Azusa Pacific Christian University where she was selected as a peer counselor for her dormitory and graduated Magna Cum Laude (beliefs and values). Heather is a unique member of God's family as marked in her gift of "gathering skills" with people (her opinions about people and relationships). She is earnestly continuing graduate school to gain a doctorate degree in psychology – wanting to serve people, while she also substitute teaches part-time (responsibilities). Heather loves life, enjoys painting, playing the piano and singing (opinions and feelings). She has dated widely and is currently engaged to a wonderful youth pastor. Dreams of home and family interface her plans (values). While she is definitely a boundaried, unique person, Heather has an identical twin, Jennifer.

Jennifer, also 23, is equally lovely and blessed with beauty. Though also petite, she was very active in sports in high school, being called "cannon-arm" as third baseman in varsity softball. Jenni can be counted on to bond easily with others and was awarded "Best Personality" her senior year (values people and working hard). Most significantly, she was awarded the "Highest Character Trophy" in her Christian high school (beliefs). She also graduated from Azusa Pacific Christian University with Cum Laude after having served as a peer counselor (values). Jenni is, despite her closeness and similarities to her twin sister, a unique and boundaried member of God's family. She displays a sensitivity to others and uses her musical abilities, vocal, piano and guitar, and her leadership skills to further Christ's body and kingdom (values and opinions). She is an elementary teacher and a new bride, serving with her youth pastor husband, Jacob, in Oregon (responsibilities). They both plan to attend graduate school for further training in psychology (values and responsibilities).

Socially both daughters have dated primarily Christians and have had, as Heather would say, "a blast." Each has been morally pure and continued to wear a purity ring, received at age 13, replacing it only with the purity of a wedding ring. Jennifer and Heather began their walk with Christ as small children and each made a significant commitment, at age 16, to spend time with God in His Word daily (beliefs and values). This has been the foundation for their steadiness. As a parent, I have not seen this daily time falter – though late dates, camping or other distractions tempt. Two consistent habits in both of the women have given their parents peace and joy. When we visited their college dorm rooms, and later their single home with their other roommates, we consistently saw both their prayer journals and Scriptures being used by their bedsides, plus the current week's memory verse. There was evidence of their time spent in His power and grace (values). Jennifer continues this practical discipline and worship in her married home, as does her husband Jacob (opinion and responsibility). This time of bonding with God and yet becoming more boundaried people – by taking the time to build and commit to their beliefs and values – have brought much happiness to our daughters and to us.

Chip, 17, is a Senior at Desert Christian High School and Student Body President, football captain, Homecoming King, 6'2" and lean (his values). He is a handsome young man with an easy manner, friendly, and attracts little children like bees, with wrinkles of his nose and winks of his eyes (opinions and feelings about people and children). Chip made an early commitment of his life to Christ and has continued a growing faithfulness to Him (beliefs). Whether he loves football, making all-county league, or music more would be hard to tell. He plays piano for the church each Sunday with a small band and enjoys writing both music and lyrics. He is known for his Christian testimony in his high school and chooses a morally pure walk (values).

Chip is in the developmental stage (according to Erikson) of discerning who he is – developing his BVORs. This is happening as he strengthens his boundaries. He recently expressed, "I was thinking the meaning of life is to serve God and help others, so maybe being a psychiatrist is a way I could do that" (beliefs and values). He plans to enter college in the fall, in preparation for medical school (responsibilities to support himself and serve others).

Sincere bonding, both vertically with God and horizontally with family and mankind is evident in this family, and provides stability and joy. Yet we honestly confess that we are still in process and truly have our moments of painful relationship adjustments in both bonding and boundaries.

When I was in the early stages of my Marriage, Family and Child Counseling practice, I questioned myself, as to my effectiveness, because I had not experienced a traumatic background of sorrow and confusion. Neither had my husband or three children. None of us had suffered or were recovering from the ravages of divorce, abortion, alcoholism, drugs, immorality or such sadnesses. Yet, I was to deal with acute suffering, with compassion and wisdom every day. Additionally, I had been asked to be the associate director of the Minirth/Meier Psychiatric Inpatient Clinic in Palm Springs. I would have both the privilege and responsibility for doing intense work with many wonderful, yet hurting people. There, a fellow Christian psychiatrist, Dr. Alan Doran, helped me sort out my particular thrust; I would minister from a position of strength, of what has worked in a family, rather than serving from a position of recovery, as some of my apt colleagues could do. My posture, though limited, appears to have been effective, as we see families healing and growing in their relationships. We humbly attempt to figure out and communicate what, other than the miraculous grace of God, has contributed to the happiness of one American family. We think a lot of it is bonding and boundaries.

Healthy and Unhealthy Boundaries

In the introduction, we stated that too much of a good thing could be unhealthy. This is true with boundaries, in that too many boundaries would cause a person to isolate, not take in new understandings, become stagnant – like a hermit. Their personality would also become rigid and would indeed prevent the very important bonding. No love or respect would be able to flow in or out. When a person's boundaries become so much like walls and prevent bonding, we call this a "disengaged person." This often happens in a family when the communication lines have stopped and we diagnose this as "emotional divorce."

Figure 2b
Rigid Boundaries

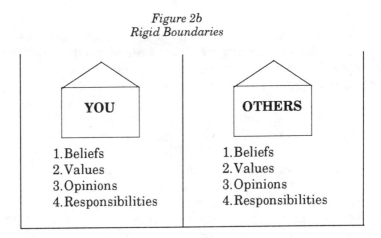

The house represents your frame, your physical self. There is much more to you than your body, but you have property – your yard – which holds your Beliefs, Values, Opinions, and Responsiblities (BVORs). Too-rigid boundaries are represented by the solid lines between you and significant others. There is no chance for communication or caring, only coexistence in loneliness (no bonding).

This may be the result of a fear of bonding (lack of trust). Or, closely connected, a person's boundaries may not have been respected; and they feel the only way to maintain their identity is to put up walls or move away from others.

We have lived next door to our same neighbors for 14 years, without conflict. The reason? We have this wonderful little two-foot-high hedge surrounding the perimeter of our property and marking where our property stops and theirs starts. We are able to see each other, share ideas, laugh and greet each other – a form of friendly bonding. We have healthy boundaries between us.

Figure 2c
Healthy, Semipermeable Boundaries

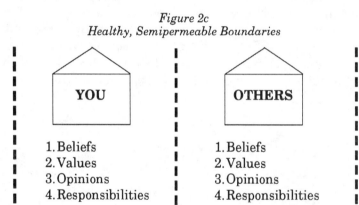

The dotted lines represent definition and protection of each person's BVORs, but allows opportunity to communicate and care about each other. This semipermeable boundary is our hedge; it allows us to live close by each other, for long periods of time, in peace and respect. It allows us to have healthy bonding.

Our neighbors have cacti and rocks in their front yard (desert style) and we, being from the Midwest, have different opinions – grass and rose trees up our walk. If because of my opinions or values I climb over my little hedge and insist on planting rose trees in their cacti patch, what will happen? Two things: one, conflict; they will not like my refusing to observe our boundary and enforcing my opinions on them, and two, while I'm busy hoeing around in their yard, my own yard will be growing weeds. And certainly the conflict will intensify if their value is that we should conserve more water. Therefore, they might climb over that little hedge, uproot our rose trees and transplant some of their cacti into our yard. Meanwhile, of course, their own responsibilities to their rock have been neglected and weeds are sprouting everywhere. If this continues and no communication resolution is applied, one of us would have to put up a "For Sale" sign and move away – this is divorce in a family. This is alienation in parent/children relationships. It is a lack of establishing and respecting one another's boundaries, thus, destroying the ability to bond, and causing walls or total pulling away from one another. It's an enmeshment of the parties which results in isolation from one another.

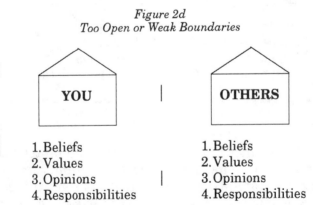

Figure 2d
Too Open or Weak Boundaries

When boundaries are weak, neither party has the strength to state and maintain boundaries that protect their own BVORs. Without definite boundaries, they climb into each other's yard, trying to fix or impose their

BVORs on them. Meanwhile, their own yard is being overtaken by weeds and needs care. Galations 6:2-5 tells us, "Each person should carry another's burden." So help others when you can and when necessary, but also, "each person should carry his own load." Maintain your own yard, with your own responsibilities. In this diagram, neither party can clearly tell the other what their BVORs are nor ask the other to respect them. This is generally because of a humungous fear of being attacked (hurt) or withdrawn from (abandoned). The result is loss of self-identity, which results in anger, depression or even resorting to Figure 2b, drawing away into isolation – loss of bonding.

Too-rigid boundaries, isolation, is as unhealthy as too open or weak boundaries – no identity. Healthy boundaries must be built and practiced, first in the family relationships, then in our extended relationships. This actually allows and aids in healthy bonding. This is clearly seen in husband-wife relationships and parent-children relationships, and then among friendships.

Figure 2e
See-Saw Balance of Bonding
and Boundaries

Bonding:
Emotional attach-
ment to others

Boundaries:
Property lines

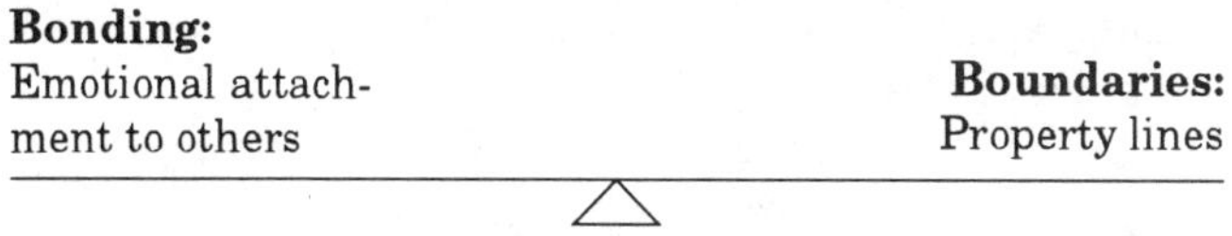

Clearly, a family needs to evaluate the delicate balance of maintaining bonding and boundaries to enhance relationships and allow individual potential. Each should have liberty to reach out and enjoy other relationships also – a healthy sign of preparing for eventual separation.

In the face of love, parents need to prepare their children to live successfully without them, autonomously. Children, big or small, need to be taught to give and receive love while respecting their parents and learning to take "no" from them, according to the parents' values. Parents, whose BVORs are clear, model to their children their boundaries and are more free to love them without resentment.

Summary

The purpose of a family is for a group of people to live together, giving and receiving love and nurturance to one another (supplying the necessary bonding). While doing this, parents are teaching BVORS and respecting, even nurturing a separateness, an individual identity, and eventual autonomy (boundaries) as the children become adults. The development of each member's beliefs, values, opinions/feelings and responsibilities provides the substance, the identity of the person, who must have a semipermeable boundary around him/her. This boundary must be defined enough to separate him/her from the general mass of the family and allow him/her to develop to his/her potential, while maintaining the important and delicate balance of connecting intimately to others in giving and taking. The experience in the family of origin is a practice ground for the offspring's future relationships in work and later his/her home. The parents have the responsibility for passing down BVORs that are godly, "bringing you (the family) the gospel, and offering you (the family) up as a fragrant sacrifice to God" (Rom. 15:16, *Living Bible*).

Reflective Questions

1. What struck you personally as you read about the crucialness of creating and maintaining boundaries in a family?

2. Do you have well-defined boundaries around you? What steps do you need to take to build them?

3. Have you allowed lack of well-defined boundaries to become walls isolating you emotionally from those you love? Are you open for learning how to make these semipermeable – a balance of bonding and boundaries?

Discussion Questions

1. Why are boundaried people the least angry people in the world?

2. If boundaries truly can be learned, what are the steps?

3. What do you need to do to develop stronger BVORs? How can you use the F.I.S.S.E.P Wheel to help you think this through?

Chapter Three

CHAPTER 3

Family Talk: Managing Anger in the Family

Families need to be a safe place, especially in their communication.

The family unit needs to be committed to safe relationships, not intentionally hurting one another by lack of love or by lack of respecting each other's individual boundaries. Home needs to be place of protection and refuge, a contrast from the torrents of the world. Whether adults or children, we can't count on our outside world to be supportive. In fact, it may be humiliating and scary. Children go to school where peers or teachers may not love them, and, indeed, they may experience isolation and disrespect for their individuality. I previously mentioned that our daughter, Heather, enjoys painting. For years she would not attempt any drawing after a teacher told her in second grade that her trees looked like a woman coming out of a hair dryer. Helping Heather regain her confidence took some family nurturance.

Husbands and wives need to be nurturing and upbuilding to each other. Adults, as well, need the soothing balm of a place of refuge after being in the battle of the world. This modeling sets a pace in the home for how everyone deserves to be treated. Husbands and wives speaking with regard for each other in the presence of their children can much more easily demand that same respect from the children. This is not to say the children cannot hear you in conflict, but better, not with an intent to hurt. Because our family members are imperfect in being a refuge for each other, it is important also to experience God as the perfect refuge.

Psalm 91:1-2 promises:

He who dwells in the shelter of the Most High, will abide in the shadow of the Almighty. I will say to the Lord, my refuge and my fortress, my God in whom I trust. (NIV)

One evening when Chip was about 8 years old, I was putting him to bed when he explained to me after prayers, "Mom, you know how I make those forts out in the backyard? That's kind of how I see Jesus. He's like a fort that I can go and hide in." In his short years, he had learned to experience God as his refuge, probably even if his family was angry with him. I later wrote out Psalm 91:1 and 2 for him on a 3 x 5 card so he could see the basis of his wisdom.

I specifically recall an afternoon when Jenni and I were in a tiff, and though I forget the reason, I can see one angry little girl (about 10) walking very briskly and stoutly through the living room, her pigtails practically flying out straight behind her. Out through the back door she marched. As she disappeared, I wondered where she might have gone and what might be so urgent for her in the backyard. Laying aside my upset, I tiptoed to the picture window to see if I could catch a glimpse of her. There she was, on a patio lawn chair, feet and knees up, supporting her Bible, where she was taking her anger before the Lord. She knew a refuge wherein she could trust. (Maybe I was unreasonable, who knows?) I was very pleased, though, because despite her irritation at me, she knew a safe refuge she could run to. She had witnessed me doing this in my moments of distress or anger. I would usually head for the bathroom, because with three children and a husband, it was the only place I could lock the door and be uninterrupted. In a family upset, she had watched me take my Bible into this solitary fortress. I would, and still do, read Psalms 39 and 40 – my personal anger chapters. Now, I was watching her find her personal refuge and fortress, where she could hide with God. What a tool for her future.

While I have confessed our communication and relationship were not and are not always "safe" to each other, and God's relationship is, safety for one another needs to be our goal. More specifically, our home needs to be a safe place to express our boundaries, our feelings, both good and bad. Our speech is given paramount importance in the Scriptures. James 3:2 says, "For we all stumble in many ways. If anyone does not stumble in what he says, he is a perfect man, able to bridle the whole body as well." Proverbs 15:1 also speaks of controlling the tongue, "A soft answer turneth away wrath: but grievous words stir up anger."

A Formula for Family Communication

Game Plan + Skilling + Practice =

Problem-Solving Communication

The game plan needs to be set, describing the rules and fouls for family talk and actions in your house. I often help families, parents and offspring, sit down and actually write these out – to be posted on the refrigerator until they are a way of life in their home. Some families say they post them in several rooms. Rules and fouls need to be discussed, suggestions given, and each rule and foul agreed upon by the group. A youngster can be the secretary to write them down after the entire family has agreed upon them. Just like in any game, if it is to be fun and enjoyable, everybody has to play by the rules or be penalized if they foul. To win at the game of family communication and relationships, everybody needs to know and buy into the rules. Then we have a chance of winning – succeeding as a family.

A set of family communication rules and fouls might look something like this:

The Game Plan

Rules

1. Everyone lower their voices when they are feeling upset, to begin to get self-control.
2. Take responsibility for what you feel and be honest to explain it.

3. Use "I" statements, in place of "You" statements. Example, "I feel put down," not "You always put me down."

4. Communicate with a mind set to solve problems, not to attack or humiliate.

5. Stick to one problem and solution, rather than listing and hopping to a list of complaints.

6. Listen... Listen... Listen... If this is difficult for some, make the 3 to 5 minute rule, where one person asks for this ruling and may speak his mind for 3 to 5 minutes without interruption. Time it.

7. Try to get in the other person's shoes as much as possible; listen to their feelings.

Others may be added as needed.

Fouls of the game of family living

1. No name-calling. Penalty: writing, "I will remember to respect people by not name-calling." The number of times can be according to the age.

2. No slamming doors or damaging property. Penalty: restoring or repairing property and/or again writing, "I need to remember that slamming doors does not solve problems, communication does."

3. No touching of any kind, not even a brush of the shoulders, when we are angry. Penalty: writing, "It is not wise to touch people when we are angered. It only inflames the anger."

4. No "shut ups." You may ask them to be quiet or to leave you alone. Penalty: writing, "I need to listen to people and set my boundaries by asking them to be quiet or by moving away from them."

Other fouls may be added and other penalties may be exchanged, such as doing extra chores, having a time out or being grounded if the writing is continually not working. We found that writing was a good way of teaching the value about which we were disciplining. As the children got into high school, sometimes we would give them a choice of their discipline, with an attitude of this being for their learning. The choice might be either to wash the front windows outside or to write a one-page essay about what was wrong with their behavior. The latter had to be without provocation, possibly supported by Scripture, and with sincere effort, indicating their remorse and true beliefs. We would never force them to do this, as we would be imposing our values onto them. However, interestingly, they usually chose the essay over a chore. Some were serious and even inspiring, others broke the ice of our tension with humor. Chip has a flare for writing. Although he gave us some humorous essays, we believe he agreed with his need to make some changes. Chip wrote the following essay for his procrastinating on cleaning up his room. He indicates no bitterness for this discipline, but did follow the rules and had the paper on my dresser before dinner. Procrastination did decrease.

My Discipline

There are, in our cursed, imperfect world, a multitude of flaws and imperfections, a major one of which is our sinful human nature. From this gaping hole in our souls often roars an ugly beast, which grasps hold of its victim in a vice-like death grip, dragging the unfortunate down into a deep pit of devilment. This monstrous troglodyte (he must have learned that legitimate word in school!) has been labeled with many names, such as disobedience, procrastination, rebellion, and more. It is necessary that this ogre be suppressed quickly at all costs due to its frightful potential to sever the life-sustaining lines of interrelational ability on a spiritual basis and the comparably trite lines between humans. In short, its destructive nature forces it to be hunted and fought with a tenacious ferocity until it is inevitably defeated.

Each of the *Family Rules and Fouls* need to be modeled, taught, and encouraged by the parents. Experientially and personally, I, Nancy, am so thankful for setting up these parameters. While we lived as a family of five, with girls and a boy, it was not necessary for them to hit each other, name call or tear things up. The penalties simply have to be consistent and more troublesome than the gain of breaking the rules. Essentially someone who is bonded to the children must consistently be in the home in order to kindly teach and enforce the game. Daily baby-sitters usually don't have that much investment in their training and future. I regularly sort out conflicts within families wherein there has been little clear game plan, and destructive relationship habits have caused damage to the family and the individuals.

During their growing up, many children have been given little practice for how they will handle people outside their home or in their future homes. This is the main point: we're teaching them in our homes how to manage outside and future relationships. While I taught school, if I observed a child stomping away and saying shut up to a teacher, while he slammed the door, I knew right away, this was what he practiced at home. If he had been taught another way to handle his frustration, he would have used it. Poor little untrained child, with no effective tools to handle his frustrations!

We need to remember that our homes are training grounds for our children's other relationships at school, at future jobs, and most crucially, their own final home. We then work on decreasing their chance of divorce. I confess that mixed in this, I have a selfish motivation. While I love my family greatly, I want to do everything I can to prevent them from moving back in our home, with their children, due to divorce. That would be a lose/lose situation for both of us. And since this is a major risk in our times, it behooves me to teach them all the skills and give them all the practice on successful human relationships I can through communication. Then if it still happens, I know I have done all I knew to do (my responsibility in my BVORs).

The Skilling (Developing and Using Needed Skills)

What then is the skill we need to add to the workable formula? We need to be able to separate *our feelings* from *what we need* (problem-solving). Bowen, a renowned social scientist, believes that 90 percent of adults cannot act out or state their feelings and needs in the face of emotion.

However, he stresses the criticalness of developing such a "differentiation" of the intellect (mind) from the emotion for successful relationships and good mental health. In other words, without clear knowledge of what I believe, value, feel, and have responsibility for, and holding it in by placing a "fence" – (boundary) around it, I will be operating by the stimulation and mercy of my own or others' emotions. Such out-of-control living causes a person to be unpredictable, even to themselves, and results in poor self-esteem. Certainly this is relevant to the Christian who is commanded to add self-control to his faith (2 Peter 1:5).

Taking responsibility for our feelings and stating them with "I statements," as previously stated in rules 2 and 3, takes practice, and even a stretch in our vocabulary. When was the last time you said honest statements like: "I feel anxious," "I feel disrespected," "I feel disappointed," "I feel helpless," "I feel betrayed," "I feel left out," or "I feel uncherished?" Whoa! We can't say those kind of honest things because:

1.   I'm not aware that's what I'm feeling; I just know I'm mad or sad – and it's probably somebody else's fault. (Faulty thinking)

2.   If I did work at knowing what was really going on with my feelings, and if I told the significant people in my life, they would probably give me a hard time. That would make me very vulnerable. In fact, they might attack me or even withdraw from me. (And I couldn't stand that.)

That kind of thinking is understandable, but leads to stuffing down your feelings and only acting them out in ineffective and often destructive ways. Feelings cannot be destroyed, but if ignored, they convert into another form. These other forms are flashing yellow lights that we are stuffing feelings. If our feelings stir around us, as if in a large balloon, and we keep a tight rubberband on our balloon, something is going to give. Ugly protrusions will pop out on the sides of our balloon. These protrusions result in pain to ourselves and to our relationships. Neither are they a sweet-smelling fragrance to our God.

Figure 3a
Our Balloon of Feelings with Ugly Protrusions
Credit: Dr. John Townsend from illustration seen in a lecture

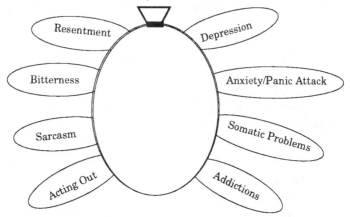

Some of us have our own special protrusion we use. Some of us use many of them.

Resentment – that killer to bonding. A person full of resentment does not tell what is really going on, but keeps a smug, unjoyful countenance; often carrying an aloof attitude and exuding anything but warmth and affirmation. Because of this, resentment appears self-righteous.

I (Nancy) confess resentment is one of my easiest ways to convert and hide my true feelings. I don't shout or cuss, but I sure know how to work this one. I feel I have replaced it with honest feelings much more these past years, but it used to be my speciality, especially if I were angry. I can remember years ago, when the children were small, standing at the kitchen sink, cleaning, but being very quiet and resentful. I may have felt used and wanted more help, but was troubled with something and converted it into resentment, instead of speaking my feelings and needs. Part of my healing was looking at what I was afraid of – the other's anger. Until I could face that, and say to myself, "That's in your yard, if you choose to be angry when I am honest," I could not follow the commandment to "live a life of love" (Eph. 5:1-2) and it robbed me and my family of joy.

Bitterness – If resentment goes on long enough, or there are enough heavy issues not dealt with, resentment turns into bitterness. Here the boundaries that need to be semipermeable and flexible in order to be healthy, now become walls. An emotional divorce takes place, a pulling away from bonding, and Satan surely has a foothold.

Sarcasm – This subtle way of expressing your feelings is indirect and has an attacking feel about it. Sarcasm generally does little more than decrease the bonding and reap resentment onto the giver. It does not usually get you what you need. A mother may say, "It's about time you came to the table, did you break your leg?" This doesn't make the child more thoughtful to her cooling dinner next time, it only antagonizes – but why does the mother do it? It keeps her less vulnerable to snap-backs. It's a hiding device, for fear of dealing with her feelings honestly. Until she faces that fear that the child may get angry or withdraw from her, and allows the child to have her own feelings, with limits on disrespectful behavior, the mother will continue to hide her feelings of being treated disrespectfully, camouflaged in sarcasm. Better than sarcasm would be: "*I feel* disrespected and frustrated when you come in for dinner 10 minutes after you've been called, and it's all cold. *I need* you to come right away or let me know if you are having a problem. If the child becomes angry or withdraws with such assertive honesty, that is not to frighten or manipulate the mother.

Acting Out – This is a specialty of adolescents because they, by virtue of their age, have so little skill in understanding their feelings or discussing their needs. They tend to just act out their feelings when the stressors get heavy. The obvious way is through getting high on drugs or alcohol. Promiscuity temporarily provides a way of escaping reality temporarily, as does shoplifting, excessive masturbating or gang activity. Therapy with adolescents stresses a teaching and encouragement to understand what they are feeling. They are taught to talk about their feelings instead of acting them out, and discuss with their families what they need.

Myra, a 14-year-old girl, living with her mother and 7-year-old brother, belligerently walked into my office. She sat down hard on my couch, folding her arms in front of her chest, and continually swung her long curly, dark hair out of her eyes. She had been sent to me for "acting out." She would cut school, get high on drugs, and be promiscuous with various boys. Her grades were a fiasco by now, and certainly her physical well-being was at grave risk with drugs and possible infectious sexual diseases. Her acting out could take her life. What was she acting out? Sessions later, as her story unfolded and we established a rapport, I invited her mother in to join us. Myra had been instructed and practiced with me to talk out her feelings to her mother, instead of acting them out. It began with her laying aside her hiding style of rebellion, and honestly telling her mother her feelings and needs. With tears and some anger, she explained to her mother, "I feel lonely when you are out so many nights a week with your boyfriends, and I need you to be home with just me, sometimes. I feel scared and frustrated. I can't make my little brother mind when you leave me with him to babysit. He threw a chair at me last time, and I hit him too hard. I need you to make him mind, and not leave him with me so much." This kind of communication, with problem-solving, was the only chance Myra had to see another way, rather than stuffing her feelings and showing Mom by acting out the next day. They needed some outside help to turn this around.

Obviously, adults also act out instead of talk out, by extramarital affairs, excessive gambling, alcohol...basically any behavior we use to replace dealing with our feelings, that is destructive to ourselves and others.

Addictions – This is closely related to acting out, but here the behavior of acting out has caught us, and the habit or physical need has made it very difficult to just drop this faulty acting out. At the root of addictions, is replacing bonding to safe people and to God with bonding to something that is a pseudo or counterfeit love. We *will* bond to something, and addictions are a harmful, counterfeit bonding. If we are not bonded in meaningful human relationships, and we are not in a love relationship with our Creator, we will bond to something else less uplifting. Food is an ever-present temptation to be that bond; the rampant eating disorders of binging and or purging represent people who are not dealing with the feeling of loneliness (see *Love Hunger*, by Minirth/Meier for further treatment of the subject). Excessive T.V. watching, soaps, overspending, sex addiction, even religiosity, and certainly codependency on one person, are some of the more subtle addictions as are the obvious ones of drugs and alcohol.

Rage – Uncontrolled anger outbursts, desires to break things, hitting, and hurting people are things that clearly depict someone whose daily feelings are being stuffed under the rug, only to erupt at unpredictable times. Rage is also a manipulation of others to keep their feelings stuffed "or else." The hidden message when we hit and break things is, their face could be next. This, then, kills honest communication, and so it kills bonding. It, like the illustration in sarcasm, has to be faced and dealt with.

Depression – Depression is often defined as anger turned inward toward yourself. Again, without acknowledging and expressing your angry feelings, they generally turn in as deep resentment and anger toward yourself. A person suffering from depression feels hopeless, apathetic, without zest for life, often gets too much sleep or wakefulness, too much eating or not enough, and is irritable. There are reasons we won't acknowledge or express those angry feelings; but basically, we find it safer and easier to stuff them down and feel depressed.

Anxiety or Panic Attacks – These symptoms dramatically mask the more important feelings. A person is usually so busy trying to alleviate the anxiety and panicky feelings, they are distracted from the real feelings that are causing them. Looking at those feelings might be scary.

Somatic Problems – The body actually reacts to the stuffing down of our feelings. Negative feelings undealt with contribute to headaches, stomach ailments, hypertension leading to heart disease, arthritis, and even cancer and viruses. Many studies report as many as 90 percent of our hospital beds are filled with ailments having emotional problems at the root. An amazing study concluded that unresolved anger and stress has six times the correlation with cancer patients as does smoking. Our antibodies are decreased by as much as 50 percent when we are depressed and stressed, making us more susceptible to viruses and colds. I have decided that I cannot afford to harbor negative feelings; I don't like to get sick.

The above describes the basic conversions we make of our negative feelings when we refuse to deal with them and resolve them. If these symptoms are dominant in your life, it is important for you to get to the root of your negative feelings. If you are not able to do this by yourself, or with friends, or in your time with God, find a Christian therapist to help you address the symptoms and more importantly the underlying stuffed feelings. *Bottom line: any of the described behaviors need to be seen as flashing yellow lights, telling us "caution, I'm stuffing feelings – what are they? And why am I stuffing?"*

The skilling, then, is first, paying attention to our feelings, getting in touch with what is going on inside us. Included here is a list of feeling words that families need to use to honestly communicate what they are actually experiencing inside. Which ones do you avoid communicating? Which ones do you need to express more often?

List of Difficult Feelings

Anger	*Anxiety*	*Depression*
Displeased	Alarmed	Depressed
Indignant	Frightened	Melancholic
Exasperated	Apprehensive	Low in Spirit
Irritated	Timid	Grieving
Annoyed	Fearful	Dejected
Troubled	Panicky	Burdened

Anger	*Anxiety*	*Depression*
Frustrated	Uneasy	Pained
Aggravated	Foolish	Sad
	Embarrassed	
	Inadequate	

Notice the words listed under anger, anxiety, and depression. I personally struggled with how should a Christian handle his/her anger? Should I even have anger, or is that bad for a Christian? I remember, years ago, standing in front of our wall-to-wall books in our den, hands on hips and looking for a book on what I should do with angry feelings when they arise. In fact, at the time I was handling it with resentment, and because I didn't confess the feelings honestly, the same ones piled up, unresolved. Ephesians 4:26 says, "When you are angry, do not sin." This began to help me acknowledge my anger as a legitimate feeling. I didn't have to sin because I was angry, I simply had to deal with it. I could use the skilling: separate my feelings from what I needed, and communicate this to my significant others. *A major principle here is: you cannot force a particular person to answer your needs; you may have to enlist other people and seek other godly ways to answer your needs.* If you feel lonely and the other person you wish to fix your loneliness doesn't want to, even though you have told him your feelings and what you need, you may need to find other godly relationships to answer your needs rather than try to demand it from that particular one or try to control him. This is decreasing codependency. Many times others are more responsive when they are not feeling forced.

To Develop This Skill:

Look at the list of feelings, acknowledge the full range of emotion, and express each type as needed.

1. Emotions need to be framed in *I feel*...rejected, threatened, lonely, angry or whatever.

This is essential in building good family communication. We need to realize and believe that feelings just are, they are not to be judged as either good or bad, but something that comes up in us, like a hiccup. We may not like them, but pushing them down gives us a stomachache – or something (the list of protrusions on page 66).

If, however, we stay stuck in what we feel and do not move to the second part of the skilling, we complain and become negative or whiney – the helpless child position. As adults, and even mature children, we must take responsibility for having that feeling and consider what it would take for us to decrease it.

2.   Emotions can then be expressed in (because I feel...) Therefore, *I need*...some attention or affirmation or time to take a walk with you or whatever.

This is part of my responsibilities within my boundaries, to problem solve my feelings and to know what I need. In fact, the term Bowen uses for this is "self-differentiation." The word basically means differing out our emotions from our intellect – our feelings from what we need (problem-solving). He even puts it on a scale:

Figure 3b
Scale of Self-Differentiation, by Bowen

0__5__10_____80__85_____100

At this end of the scale, a person is poorly self-differentiated. He is at the mercy of his emotions.

If he is:

angry – he gets enraged or sulks

sad – he gets depressed or withdrawn

anxious – he gets panicky or avoidant (as examples)

At this end of the scale, a person is highly self-differentiated. He is able to separate his emotions from his intellect. He communicates:

I feel...(therefore) I need...

Only Jesus would be at the 100 mark, perfectly self-differentiated; but a belief in my BVORs is I want to practice – learning how to live most of the time at the upper end of the scale, rather than on a 5, at the mercy of my emotions. I admit though, sometimes I shake my head at myself and say, "I acted like a minus 1 in that situation."

The lower end of the scale, the poorly self-differentiated behavior, clearly does not please the Lord; it is the antithesis of righteousness, joy and peace. These are what we are to seek to further. Our family's life verse is Matthew 6:33, "But seek ye first the kingdom of God, and His righteousness; and all these things shall be added unto you." Since this has been our goal for 27 years, I am alert to teachings about what the kingdom of God is. When I found Romans 14:17, "For the kingdom of God is not meat and drink; but righteousness, and peace, and joy," it became increasingly important for me not to live on the low end of the differentiation scale – at the mercy of my emotions. But in order to further the kingdom of God, I needed this tool of learning how to separate my feelings from my intellect, so that I could further righteousness, peace and joy in my little world. I recently used the skilling with another administrator at our hospital. I said, "I'm feeling confused about 'the plans.' I need to understand more of their purpose." We had respectful communication without complaining or attacking. I often help executives learn to use the skilling of self-differentiation in their businesses. It gives a plan for approaching problems with honesty and problem-solving.

These underlying beliefs give further unction to learn this skill of self-differentiation.

#1 "He who compresses his lips brings evil to pass" (Prov. 16:30, NIV).

The preceding list of symptoms or ugly protrusions (page 66) from resentment to addictions were described as a result of compressing the lips and stuffing down, instead of talking out. The Proverbs are filled with the wise use of the tongue. I keep a running "T" by all the verses I find on how to use the tongue, as I am convinced it is such a powerful tool to further His kingdom and my own peace and joy. Other verses wisely tell us:

Righteous lips are the delight of kings, and they love him that speaketh right (Prov. 16:13).

He that speaketh truth sheweth forth righteousness (Prov. 12:17).

Lying lips are abomination to the Lord: but they that deal truly are His delight (Prov. 12:22).

So to compress our lips and not talk, or to lie and say other than what is the truth, is not of God – and we have seen how people can act it out destructively.

#2 "Speak the truth in love" (Eph. 4: 15 and 25).

Not only are we to not repress our communication in problem-solving, using the avoidant approach, but we are to open our mouths and speak what is the truth, not with put downs and attacking or sarcasm, but in love. I see the use of the skilling of "I feel...(therefore) I need..." helpful in working out the following admonitions:

There is that speaketh like the piercings of a sword: but the tongue of the wise is health. The lips of truth shall be established forever: but a lying tongue is but for a moment (Prov. 12:18-19).

A soft answer turneth away wrath: but grievous (harsh) words stir up anger. The tongue of the wise useth knowledge aright, but the mouth of fools poureth out foolishness (Prov. 15:1-2). (Better to express what I honestly feel and ask for what I need than to play the fool and spout folly.)

The heart of the righteous studieth (ponders how) to answer: but the mouth of the wicked poureth out evil things (Prov. 15:28). (It takes pondering to honestly consider what you are feeling and express it with humility and clarity.)

The heart of the wise teacheth his mouth, and addeth learning to his lips (Prov. 16:23). (It takes learning and teaching your mouth to be highly self-differentiated – separating your emotions from your intellect.)

Let me cite some examples of implementing the skilling.

Lydia, a lovely, capable 35-year-old woman, was flashing yellow lights of anger and depression. As we uncovered some of her real feelings, she was feeling like a child in her marriage with her spouse. An example she gave me was when she was leaving with the car, her husband would say, "Do I have to take the car phone out before you use the car? You'll probably forget to lock it and it will get stolen." These continual inferences of her incapabilities had mounted to feelings of anger toward him. When she decided what the best description of their relationship was, that she felt like a child, and he was her parent, she was able to put into words:

Step 1. Know your feelings, and express, "**I feel** like a child, when you speak down to me about the car phone (think *therefore*)."

Step 2. Take personal responsibility for decreasing that negative feeling by expressing, "**I need** for you to speak to me as you would any adult, and ask or remind me, like, 'Would you be sure to close the sunroof? The phone is in the car.' "

Her opinions of how a wife should be spoken to and the role she wanted to play as an adult were being crossed – her boundaries were violated. Now that she knew what her opinions/feelings were, she could maintain her boundaries and have less anger symptoms. With time and regular clarity of explaining how this type of conversation was undermining both of their goals for intimacy (bonding), they were able to learn new ways of speaking to each other.

Many times, the clear communication of "I feel_____when_____ and therefore I need_____" resolves the problem, as people hear our earnest feelings without attack. However, often the other party has opposing and real feelings that need to be heard and followed with what they need. That leads us to step 4. (Are you asking what happened to step 3? Good, you're alert.)

Step 4. Negotiation or Compromise

Candy, a frustrated wife, displaying the symptoms of resentment and withdrawal from her husband, finally was able to state what her inside feelings were to her husband. "Since I quit working, I feel powerless, when I have to ask you for every dollar I want." (Therefore), "I need my own checkbook."

Step 1 and Step 2 were followed, but Bill, the spouse, was not willing to comply and hand her a checkbook. Previous negative balances and frustrated experiences with two checkbooks loomed in his mind. Candy needed to listen to his feelings and needs, and indeed to help him express them.

Bill expressed, "I feel anxious, even angry, when I give you a checkbook and see you have not considered the negative balance, I need to maintain one checkbook." Stalemate? No, here, both feelings and needs are legitimate and each of them needs to take responsibility for the values and opinions in their boundaries. Respecting each other's BVORs will require them to move toward negotiation, the mindset of, how can this be a win/win?

4a. Negotiation=win/win

She needs some increased power in the marriage, as seen in being able to make some choices in spending money without asking him for each dollar. He needs the security of knowing and keeping the balance in the black. When their basic feelings and needs are set out objectively, without attacking or being stuck in complaining, they can take responsibility for suggesting win/win solutions. Perhaps they could decide on an agreed-upon budgeted amount that she could spend, either in cash or in a separate checkbook. She could make spending choices within that sum, while he could thereby know the checkbook balance, having already subtracted her allowance. This acknowledges each family member's feelings and allows each one to take responsibility for a solution for his or her feelings. Each person needs to be ready for negotiation, when necessary. This works not only for husband-wife relationships, but for parent-child relationships. These skills need to be brought to the "family conference table" (to be covered shortly).

Did you remember that step 3 was skipped? It was skipped because it is the one that is best to avoid in order to have functional relationships. Nevertheless, since it is often a part of family communication, and since it is what attempts to violate each other's boundaries, we must not only discuss it, but become proficient at spotting it...

Step 3. Manipulation

Manipulation is a reaction that may happen right after Step 1, "I feel" and Step 2, "I need." The first time I worked at separating my feelings from my intellect, and expressed what I felt and what I needed, I sort of waited for an applause. I mean, I had done what the theorists say — I had self-differentiated. Yet not only was the other party not applauding, I was, in so many words, being told my feelings were inane. In short, I was being attacked. I ended in tears, totally disappointed that my wise, mature way of communicating was not working. My problem? I didn't know how to spot manipulation.

Manipulation is the effort, conscious or unconscious, to control or repress other's feelings and, certainly, their needs.

Manipulation sounds wicked, but being the wicked creatures we are, we all do it from time to time. However, a premise for a happy, peaceful family is to be trained to spot manipulation in yourself and in others, and decrease its power.

He that answereth another before he heareth it is folly and shame unto him. The spirit of a man will sustain his infirmity, but a wounded (broken)

spirit who can bear? The heart of the prudent get-
teth knowledge; and the ear of the wise seeketh
knowledge (Prov. 18:13-14).

The manipulating person does not listen to the feelings of others but breaks their spirit. The wise person
strives for the goal of knowing others' feelings and understanding them.

A wise, experienced Christian couple came to me for
premarital counseling. Each had been through the ravages of divorce and were concerned about not repeating
earlier mistakes. I will never forget their opening statement, "We don't want to control or to be controlled. We
learned that in our first marriages." They were talking
about manipulation – one controlling the other.

Manipulation has two faces to watch for: *Attack* and
Withdrawal.

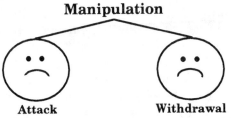

Manipulation

Attack   **Withdrawal**

Falling under the category of these faces are statements of:

- Blame
- Rage
- Threat
- Minimizing
- Ignoring
- Out-talking or Over-talking
- Disqualifying what you feel

Attack is obvious to see. Yet, as I confessed, I did not
recognize it as the normal manipulation that often follows
conveying your feelings and asking for what you need. If
we do not spot the attacking as manipulation, we allow it
to enter our boundaries and into our feelings. We then re-

press the expression of our beliefs, values, opinions or responsibilities, our BVORS. Our feelings will not disappear, but take on another form, as explained earlier (the protrusions, page 66).

For example, remember when Bill expressed himself about feeling anxiety and anger over the checkbook having a minus balance? Candy could have answered him with, "You're just a chauvinist, wanting all the control!" This would have been a way of her trying to manipulate him by attack. His best response, to decrease the power of manipulation, would have been:

a. To recognize this as a manipulating gesture.

b. The manipulation was to try to invalidate his feelings of worrying about an overdrawn checkbook.

c. She was using the face of anger to get him to "stuff down" his feelings that threatened she might have to change.

d. Therefore, he, seeing this manipulation, could choose to let it roll off of his back, and continue to honestly admit his feelings of anxiety and anger.

e. He could attempt to hear her honest feelings.

f. They could move toward a negotiation.

The sooner we understand that everyone will, at some time, try to manipulate us, the closer we can get to solutions. We can then forgive them for it but be responsible for our own feelings. It's like remembering to hoe in your own yard by dealing with your own feelings, without climbing over in their yard to hoe out their manipulation.

The other face of manipulation is withdrawal. This is more subtle. These manipulators generally do not even know they are doing it. They just know the behavior has worked before and, in fact, have probably watched their parents do it. They may, inadvertently, have become an expert at it, simply by watching it for 18-plus years.

In the case of Lydia, when she told her husband honestly, "I feel like a child when you speak to me in a put-down manner," if he had chosen to be manipulative by withdrawal, he could have simply given the cold shoulder – for days. He could have been silent at the dinner table, turned over in bed without hardly a kiss good-night, barely spoke the next day – all in a conscious or most likely, an unconscious effort, to manipulate her into never confronting him again with her feelings and needs. If she recanted on her feelings, and said, "Oh, Honey, I'm sorry for being grumpy," in order to get his cheerfulness back or his warmth to her, she would reinforce his behavior of withdrawal manipulation. Worse yet, she may repress any feelings she has next time, and just go overeat or push it into somatic physical problems or even a flirtation. "Repressed lips bring forth evil" (Prov. 16:30). If he manipulates, she needs to forgive the manipulation, leaving it in his yard, stay by her feelings and relate to other safe, godly people while he is in his manipulative state of withdrawal, thereby decreasing its power.

Principle: As long as manipulation works, it continues.

The formula then, for family communication is:

Game Plan + Skilling + Practice =
Problem-Solving Communication

To teach and implement the game plan takes practice in verbalizing the skilling, self-differentiation, without manipulative controlling. But the results are well worth the righteousness, peace, and joy it brings, and are a sweet-smelling fragrance to God. And since the results of that action further God's kingdom (Rom. 14:17), He will help us if we ask Him, and we will reap eternal joys.

A final tool for family communication is the *Family Conference Table*. This is a time of communication around the family table. It can be called by anyone in the family for a particular time. Or you may set a special evening after dinner to have one regularly. The Game Plan and the Skilling must be the norms. A practical plan to have established is that if, during the family conference, someone is crossing my boundaries and ignoring my BVORs (bottom line, I'm getting very upset), I may rise momentarily, signifying I need some "backing off" of the honest communication. This is to be respected, since the family is to be a safe place for communication, not a place where we are beat down. Family conference tables aim for empathy of each person's feelings and move toward problem solving. This is an excellent place to model and teach the legitimacy of feeling and the skilling of "I feel...therefore, I need." An especially nice touch is to end family conference tables with a dessert or special treat of doing something everyone likes, such as getting a video or going out for frozen yogurt.

Summary

Families need to be a safe place for each of the members to express their feelings and their needs. The formula for effective family communication is:

Game Plan + Skilling + Practice =
Problem-Solving Communication

The game plan needs to be set, describing the rules, fouls, and penalties for how your family is going to talk and act. The steps for executing the skilling are:

Step 1. Know your feelings, and express, "**I feel...**"

Step 2. Take personal responsibility for decreasing that negative feeling by expressing, "**I need...**"

Step 3. Spot **manipulation** as seen in attack or withdrawal; forgive it and let it remain in the other person's yard, while you stay by your feelings, ready to listen to their feelings and needs.

Step 4. Negotiation. Aim for a win/win, as each person's feelings and needs are considered.

Feelings cannot be destroyed, but when repressed, convert into destructive modes of behavior, often known as sin. Speaking the truth in love promotes righteousness, peace and joy, thus furthering God's kingdom.

Reflective Questions

1. Is your family a safe place for each member's feelings to be shared? Do you have an established *Game Plan* for communication?

2. Is the full range of emotion (anger, anxiety, and sadness) allowed in your home?

3. Which of the four steps in the skilling are the most difficult for you? for your family members?

Discussion Questions

1. How can you make your family a safer place for your family members to express their honest feelings?

2. Discuss how the goal of being higher on the scale of self-differentiation can help your family further the kingdom of God, that of righteousness, peace and joy.

3. How could "compressing your lips" bring forth evil in your family? How could "speaking the truth in love" make your family have a sweeter fragrance before God?

Chapter Four

CHAPTER 4

God's Expectations of the Wife and Husband – Goals and Roles

Relationships in our homes is the entity that has the power to bring either glory to God or grief to God. Most important is the husband-wife relationship. The marriage relationship has three major components: the husband, the wife, AND the relationship.

Roger and Rita sat across from each other in the wing-backed chairs in my office. While they had been married 15 years, it was clear they were emotionally isolated and vastly different in their individual moods. Rita began the explanation of their scenario. "Mrs. Dean, I believe there's something you can't quite understand. You see, I love God with my whole heart. There is nothing more important to me than Him."

I quickly empathized, "Oh, I think I can understand, I too have given my life to Christ, since a child, and He is my Lord."

Rita continued, "No, you see, He is everything to me. And I don't care about worldly interests like my husband does. I only care about what God wants of my life."

Roger's face was the picture of disappointment, discouragement, and general grief. He began to disclose his feelings of hurt over Rita's criticism of him not being college educated, but being a blue-collar worker. He lamented of the efforts he had made to relate to Rita, such as buying tickets for special events, wherein she gave them away to neighbors – too much of a waste of her time when she could be studying the Word. She had returned an anniversary ring he bought her, to use the money for something else she wanted. Tears filled his eyes when he described their evenings, with Rita shut up in her bedroom, engrossed in her books, telephone, and music. For years, Rita had not allowed him any affection, while she kept herself very attractive and busy attending the various religious meetings she enjoyed.

Dear Rita had missed a very important concept in her understanding of Christianity. There was another entity in their home, besides her and her husband – the relationship. Rita did not conceive of the idea that their relationship was an important third, living, energy in their home, that could bring delight to God or grieve Him. I showed them the following diagram of a marriage.

Figure 4a
H=Husband; W=Wife; R=Relationship

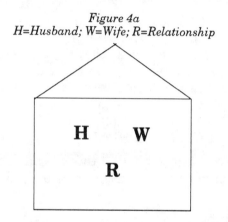

I described the relationship as an unseen, but important, entity in their marriage. It could be compared to a baby of theirs. If it were cared for, nurtured, and treated tenderly, it could be strong and healthy. This dependent's welfare is gravely affected by the care the other residents in the marriage give to it. The relationship's health must be regularly monitored, watching for symptoms of discouragement, distancing, anger, depression, apathy, boredom, resentment, acting out, and – a big one – lack of verbal expression of feelings and needs. The husband and wife must make problem-solving plans for any of these symptoms. Then the relationship's health will be guarded and preserved. If such symptoms continue to flash yellow warning lights and no care is given, the dependent relationship may die or, at best, struggle on, sickly and dysfunctional.

This baby, their relationship, was what had the power to emit the "sweet smelling sacrifice" to their heavenly Father. The sad end of this story was: Rita was not interested in caring for this unseen member of their family, only herself and her somewhat distorted understanding of God.

There are times when couples will have to expend energy for the relationship's health, doing things that they, in their natural capacity, have no desire to do, either because of irritation, disappointment or just apathy. Basically, God tells us over and over to live a life of love (Eph. 5:1). While our individual character is important, it is best revealed in our relationships with others. Our relationships, again, have an enormous power to please God or grieve God.

> Don't cause the Holy Spirit sorrow by the way you live. Remember, He is the One who marks you to be present on that day when salvation from sin will be complete. Stop being mean, bad-tempered and angry. Quarreling, harsh words, and dislike of others should have no place in your lives. Instead, be kind to to each other, tenderhearted, forgiving one another, just as God has forgiven you because you belong to Christ. Follow God's example in everything you do just as a much-loved child imitates his father. Be full of love for others, following the example of Christ, who loved you and gave himself to God as a sacrifice to take away your sins. And God was pleased, for Christ's love for you was like a sweet perfume to him (Eph. 4: 30–5: 2, *Living Bible).

I, personally, as a wife, am regularly called into mental accountability to assess what the aroma of our marital relationship is before God. Does it bring Him sorrow or pleasure? In the beginning of this book, we presented bonding and boundaries as practical and helpful tools to benefit and improve significant relationships. In consideration of the husband-wife relationship, let us now see the value of applying the principles of bonding and boundaries.

The Boundaries of a Husband and Wife – Their Self-Definitions

If spouses do not feel whole in themselves or developed in their self-definitions, each may try to compensate for this by being controlling or bossy with their mate. Because they have not developed their own property lines and responsibilities, spouses sometimes tend to hoe in the other person's yard, causing damage to the other's flower garden and, thereby, provoking them. Manipulation runs rampant without respect for property lines. Each one may actually believe that they are to control the other one, while their own self-control is minimal. The wife may outwardly display a submissive lifestyle, while inwardly resenting her role and stuffing her strong feelings of desire to be free to pursue her individual development. The husband may fail to exert leadership in the home because his own self-definition is not developed.

When spouses, female or male, feel confident and clear about what their beliefs, values, opinions and feelings are concerning their spousal role, and they are free to act on them, then they are able to bond more intimately. Research indicates that in the stages of emotional development, intimacy depends upon a clear development of one's identity. The development of a clear identity is knowing one's own boundaries. Each person is a whole person when his and her self-identity is developed, that is, when their BVORs are clear. This is not to say that our BVORs are established once and for all. They are not. We mature and change, and our BVORs change. However, at any one point in life a clear understanding of our BVORs enables us to know who we are at that point in time. The husband with a clear self-identity, then, is able to confidently assert what he believes, values, feels, and has responsibility for, and can take leadership. The wife, with the development of her boundaries, is then more able to verbalize and live by her beliefs, values, opinions and responsibilities – in other words, to be herself.

A problem now becomes apparent. If both husband and wife have clear self-definitions, what if they have conflicting beliefs, values, and opinions? Sparks may begin to fly as two unmovable objects constantly clash. This conflict is not all bad even though it may be painful. Appropriate tending to conflict in the relationship can be very helpful. No one person has beliefs, values, and opinions that are perfectly mature or accurate. The conflict and adjustment to each other may necessitate adjustment of the BVORs on the part of both the husband and the wife, hopefully toward more maturity. We compare marriage to a pressure cooker. In a pressure cooker the food is subjected to intense pressure to change it in order to make it more palatable. The pressure of conflict in a marriage relationship can produce change in the husband-wife relationship and in each one's character. These changes can make them and their marriage more savory to God.

We are suspicious of couples who say they never fight. That may indicate that one is overpowering the other and the dominant one is imposing his or her beliefs, values, opinions, and responsibilities on the other. The other one is overly submissive and, in the process, has not developed or has lost a clear sense of who they are, what they value and believe, and what their opinions and responsibilities are. We know a married couple who has been married for many years. The husband is a very dominant man and will not tolerate any disagreement from his wife. If she expresses an opinion contrary to his, he responds with anger. This anger has intimidated his wife for the many years of marriage to the point that she rarely expresses any opinion that is contrary to that of the husband. If you ask her what she believes about the election that recently took place, she parrots the opinion of her husband. They do not fight much. But in the process, she has surrendered her self-identity that is defined by her beliefs, values, opinions, and responsibilities. She has not only stuffed her feelings, she has abandoned them and herself in the process.

People with an undeveloped self-identity tend to draw other people with like undeveloped self-identity. This might be masked by one appearing more domineering and the other subservient; whereas two whole people, who know what they believe, value and have responsibility for, tend to draw to each other and serve one another, thus fulfilling Ephesians 5:21, "Submitting yourselves one to another in the fear of God."

The more each person's BVORs are founded in the teachings of God's plan for husbands and wives, obviously, the better the chance for success in the marriage, which is God's institution. Let us look, then, at the beliefs, values, and opinions of a husband and wife as God directs them to be.

Within the Husband's /Wife's Boundaries — Beliefs

Men and women marry for many reasons: security, approval from society and family, to have babies, to avoid loneliness, for fun, to satisfy the sexual drive, or to have their own home...to name only a few. While these are normal motivations to seek a mate, these should not supersede the belief that God desires that this relationship develop into marriage in order to bring glory to Him. As a child of God, I am to marry someone with similar BVORs, one with whom I can more richly carry out my commitment to serve and love God with all my heart, soul, and mind. The Christian's beliefs and values should be in accord with God's intentions for His people. A commitment of marriage should not undo one's first commitment to love and serve God. Ideally then, an unwed man or woman of God would be selecting a mate with whom each could "plow the field of life" with effectiveness because they have similar beliefs, values, opinions, and responsibilities. This is some of the thought behind our Lord's command: "Be ye not unequally yoked together with unbelievers" (2 Cor.

6:14). Since Jesus was speaking to an agrarian culture, one that used yoked oxen to plow their fields, this makes more of an impact if we consider the following setting.

Figure 4b
The Fields of Life: Equally Yoked and Unequally Yoked

I envision the field as life, and my goal of plowing it as the purpose of mankind, that of bringing glory to God. If I am as the oxen who plowed in the biblical days, it will be easier for me to accomplish my task of plowing (bringing glory to God), if my yoke is adjusted with an oxen of similar beliefs. I may still be able to accomplish the task unequally yoked, but the rows may not be as straight, and it will be more difficult for me. However, if I am already married and my mate is not a believer, then my goal is still the same – to bring glory to God with my life and my marital relationship. First Corinthians 7:13-14 commands me not to skip out on the relationship, but to love that mate that he (or she) might be won to Christ. My mother is an example of this. While still young, she married my father, who was a good man but not committed to Christ. For many unhappy years she believed that she could not make that relationship bring glory to God, because she had married "out of the will of God" – unequally yoked. She later changed that attitude and tried to make the most of the situation and attempted to glorify God in her situation. It was not ideal but much happier and I'm sure more pleasing to God. Her new commitment paid off as my father subsequently received Christ and was baptized at 72 years of age. They lived their latter years with much more happiness. Most importantly, their relationship was a sweeter fragrance and glorified God.

Each spouse's beliefs, then, can be summed up with his or her commitment to live his or her role, as a husband or wife, that would bring glory to God. Each should set his or her mind to do God's will in the marriage and to have the main ambition to "find out what pleases the Lord" (Eph. 5:10, NIV). "Therefore, also we have as our ambition, whether at home or absent, to be pleasing to Him" (2 Cor. 5:9, NIV).

The Values of the Husband/Wife

Values, again, are what is really important to us. They are what we love, where we are willing to put our energy, time, and even our money. In a world where there is so much information, propaganda, and media telling us what is the best way to live, what is right or wrong, a Christian marriage needs to value the Word of God as the authority for faith and practice. Every couple needs to love God's Word, bow to its authority, and grow in their understanding and obedience to it. Without this authority for them, the relationship cannot appropriately be tended, and unresolvable conflict may result.

While this is true about all areas of life – such as use of the tongue, use of our money, and many other practical topics of life – the role of the husband and wife as outlined in the Scriptures is sometimes the most misconstrued. The selfishness of either one can cause him or her to interpret it for their best interest, neglecting the paramount law of love. First Peter 3:8-12 sums up his exhortation to both husband and wife with:

> Finally, be ye all of one mind, having compassion one of another, love as brethren, be pitiful, be courteous: Not rendering evil for evil, or railing for railing: but contrariwise blessing; knowing that ye are thereunto called, that ye should in-

herit a blessing. For he that will love life, and see good days, let him refrain his tongue from evil, and his lips that they speak no guile: Let him eschew evil, and do good; let him seek peace, and ensue it. For the eyes of the Lord are over the righteous, and his ears are open unto their prayers: but the face of the Lord is against them that do evil.

Husbands and wives need to value what God's Word teaches, as opposed to self-righteousness or selfish ideology. God delineates responsibilities for each, to be covered under that topic. First, a couple has to value the whole Word of God as their guideline for how to interact.

The Opinions/Feelings of the Husband and Wife

The Husband

A Christian husband, according to the Word of God, needs to consider the relationship with his wife of paramount importance and as a way to delight His Lord. In 1 Peter 3:7, God addresses the husbands:

> Likewise ye husbands, dwell with them (your wives) according to knowledge (the *Living Bible* calls it "being thoughtful of their needs"), giving honor unto the wife, as unto the weaker vessel, and as being heirs together of the grace of life; that your prayers be not hindered.

Our friend, Drew, in Chapter One, did not have this opinion and feeling to understand his wife's emotional struggles. Honor and respect for her as an equal is inherent in this bold teaching in a time when the society considered a wife little more than the property of the man. While women's rights movements have affected society's opinions on the equality of men and women, only God can fill the heart of a husband with the love, tenderness, and respect that the soul of a woman yearns for. We need a work of the Holy Spirit in our lives to love another person unconditionally as Christ loved us, whether their behavior motivates it or not.

Husbands, love your wives, even as Christ also loved the church, and gave himself for it; that he might sanctify and cleanse it with the washing of water by the word, that he might present it to himself a glorious church, not having spot, or wrinkle, or any such thing; but that it should be holy and without blemish (blameless). So ought men to love their wives as their own bodies. He that loveth his wife loveth himself. For no man ever yet hated his own flesh; but nourisheth and cherisheth it, even as the Lord the church; For we are members of his body, of his flesh, and of his bones. For this cause a man shall leave his father and mother, and shall be joined unto his wife, and they two shall be one flesh. This is a great mystery: but I speak concerning Christ and the church. Nevertheless let every one of you in particular so love his wife even as himself (Eph. 5:25-33).

Seldom do we see stories in our modern media that glorify such instruction and beliefs. Often the gist of the plot is, if your passions lead you astray, "whatcha gonna do?" Or if it gets too hard, live in an emotional divorce, wherein the couple maintains the home together for financial reasons, social face or the children. Repenting of self-centeredness and working at loving each other, by the grace of God, does not seem to sell too many movies lately.

In contrast, some lives around us do depict such Christlike love. Recently, it came to our attention that a president of a well-respected Christian college announced his resignation from his prominent position. His reason? He explained he felt God was calling him to stay home more and care for his wife who had Alzheimer's disease. The symptoms of that disease decrease the bonding ability and mental stimulation a person can give to another person, and generally include a strong element of irritability. This decision must have been made with the motivation of "loving his wife." These lives inspire us to see the practicalness of God's teaching.

The Wife

A husband's belief that it is right for him to love his wife will do little good if the wife's opinion is not that this is meaningful for her. In our era, many "golden apples" allure the wife to find fulfillment. Truly she has more opportunity to develop herself, if she desires, than at any other period. And this is not only a benefit to society, but has become a cultural issue, with the advent of birth control and smaller families. The woman generally does not bear and rear children until near her death as she did in the past, but, instead, has several decades of living with little or no physical obligation to children. Often, her energies are needed to help make the money for the children's college or to help prepare the couple for retirement. The debate as to whether wives should work outside of the home has supported many a discussion. The bottom line is, if we encourage a man to include in the opinions of his boundaries to not only love his wife, but to leave his father and mother and to cleave to her, the wife needs to have, in her opinions and feelings, the appreciation of his love. She needs to be available for not only receiving his love, but for nurturing it and returning it.

Many couples come into my office in marital stress, primarily because they have scheduled out or deleted time to love and play together. The priorities of making a living, perhaps both working, and the care of children, have left little or no energy or creativity for their relationship. Their feelings for one another have grown cold and, worse yet, often pained because of the treatment they have received at the hand of the other.

This surely is not all caused by the woman's desire to develop herself. Most families demand for the husband to work (Mr. Moms are yet in the minority), and when both the husband and wife are intent on their work, exhausted by its demands, many times no one is in the position to tend the home fires or encourage love to be given or received. Being a professional person myself, I do not advocate that wives remain undeveloped, but a wife does need to maintain the feeling of enjoying her husband's love and having the spirit of being loveable, in addition to expressing love to him.

First Peter 3:3-4 describes this as:

Whose adorning let it not be that outward adorning of plaiting the hair, and of wearing of gold (jewelry), or of putting on of apparel; but let it be the hidden man of the heart, in that which is not corruptible, even the ornament of a meek and quiet spirit, which is in the sight of God of great price.

This, I know, is a challenge, whether the wife is under the pressure of being home with little children or out in the work force. Maintaining as a priority, the opinion and soft, warm feelings about receiving and giving love in regard to her husband – seeking bonding – is the mainstay of the home. The wife has a unique make up for gentling and softening the ambience of the home, if it's her opinion and feelings to do so. Being cherished by her husband will help her form such an opinion.

Every wise woman buildeth her house: but the foolish plucketh it down with her hands (Prov. 14:1).

This is a convicting verse for women. I have often envisioned myself tearing the pictures off the wall, ripping the wallpaper, and wrecking my lovely home. This is what I am figuratively doing if I am foolish by being grumpy or unlovable rather than building my home by promoting love and care.

We have looked at the importance of the wife having the opinion and feelings for nurturing a home, including husband, atmosphere, and children. These are her bonding issues. The balance would be her boundaries. Here she needs also to express her feelings of emotional needs, lest she act them out in unloving ways. She also needs to express her feelings and opinions about wanting to develop herself, whether that is in the home with projects and services or outside the home in a career. I have witnessed many women who suffered from depression, largely due to their inability to express their feelings and needs to their husbands, and press for changes in their homes that would allow them to develop themselves. These women play the victim or helpless child role, with their husband playing the authoritarian father role – not what God describes in His Word for husbands and wives.

The Responsibilities of a Husband: From a Pastor's Point of View

A Husband Must Regard His Wife as a Person, Not as Property

The fall of humankind had tremendous impact on husband-wife relationships, as did the atonement of Christ. The enemy and the world system cannot be pinpointed as the only source of evil that has historically resulted in the oppression of women (see Chapter 8). This would be too easy on men and absolve them of their responsibility regarding sin. The sin nature that humankind inherited from Adam is still present. Paul accounts for our propensity to sin: "Wherefore, as by one man sin entered into the world, and death by sin: so death passed upon all men, for that all have sinned" (Rom. 5:12). Often our sin nature prompts us to do enough damage on our own without the help of the evil one. Paul describes what it does:

> For the flesh lusteth against the Spirit, and the Spirit against the flesh: and these are contrary the one to the other: so that ye cannot do the things that ye would. But if ye be led of the Spirit, ye are not under the law. Now the works of the flesh are manifest, which are these; Adultery, fornication, uncleanness, lasciviousness, Idolatry, witchcraft, hatred, variance, emulations, wrath,

strife, seditions, heresies, Envyings, murders,
drunkenness, revellings, and such like: of the
which I tell you before, as I have also told you in
time past, that they which do such things shall
not inherit the kingdom of God (Gal. 5: 17-21).

Humankind cannot contend that the only explanation
for our sin is that: "The Devil made me do it." As with
Adam, we in our Adamic nature have the incredible ability
to take something beautiful and mess it up. This is what
we have done with the male-female relationship. The oppressive system of this fallen world, coupled with our sin
nature, has been integrated into the shattered relationship between man and woman, resulting in man's
oppression of women. Since we still live in this oppressive
system and since we still have the sin nature, we in the
church must be alert to theology that perpetuates oppression of women since such oppression is diametrically opposed to Christ's atoning work wherein He has given wom-
en equal status with men. We must be particularly alert to
this oppression in the male-female sexual relationship.

As L.W. Countryman develops the theme that women
and children in the ancient world are property, he says
that: "Property denotes something which is understood as
an extension of the self, so that a violation of my property
is a violation of my personhood." Before a woman was
married she was the property of her father. She became
her husband's property at the time of betrothal. G. Bilezikian points out that: "Since a married man was ruler
over his wife, her unfaithfulness violated his property
rights." Sexual violation of her was not so much the violation of a person as it was a violation to the property. The
Torah (the first five books of the Bible, written by Moses)
emphasized this lowly position of a woman. L.W. Countryman reviews the law:

A priest was allowed to mourn only for members
of his immediate family, and this included neither
his wife nor his married sister (Lev. 21: 1-4).

A woman never became truly a member of her

husband's family, since she could be separated from it through divorce. The Torah gave the right of divorce only to the husband, preserving a unique power to him in the relationship (Deut. 24: 1-4). To be deprived of the right of divorce was a serious punishment.

The power of the father and then of the husband meant that a woman could enjoy at most, only a secondary role in whatever household she belonged to. In fact, her position could be worse than just secondary. The ideal for a woman was to be a wife, but many found themselves in various grades of slavery, while even those who had achieved the status of wife might lose it through divorce or widowhood.

This lowly position for the woman was the result of the fall of humankind which included the domination of the man over the woman and the shattering of their relationship so that anything but love governed that relationship (Gen. 3:16). Since the woman was regarded as property, it becomes apparent why the sexual ethic was as it was. It also becomes apparent that if woman was viewed as being in an egalitarian relationship with man, she could no longer be regarded as property and sexual treatment of her would have to change. Forced sexual relations with a woman would become more than the violation of another man's property; it would become the violation of the woman as a person.

In our twentieth century and in the context of sexual ethics, have we escaped this concept that a woman is a piece of property? Absolutely not. One example is the "tailhook" party that took place in Las Vegas in which United States male naval aviator officers sexually degraded other female naval personnel by forcing them to strip, and who knows what else. Also, a Los Angeles Times article (March 23, 1992) told of the sons of five prominent families in Tampa, Florida, who after "dosing" a 22-year-old woman with LSD and while she was unconscious violated her with various objects, jeering and taking photos. They did not think they were doing anything wrong in that they were not hurting her. One of the defense attorneys for the men said: "The activities that were described in the trial are commonplace. And it does not worry me. People should be allowed to engage in whatever sexual activity they desire as long as it's not violent. And I believe that's what we had here." One of the men testified, without remorse, that the only thing that marred the fun in the bedroom that night was when one of his companions leaped off the bed and broke a nightstand. That nightstand was a piece of property that was valued above a woman. The woman, to them, was property that had less value than that of a nightstand. These are only two incidents that illustrate that the degradation of women is still with us.

Are traces of this ancient world's view of women as property still impacting marriages – Christian marriages? This attitude manifests itself in teaching that sets forth an unbalanced hierarchical male-female relationship and unduly focuses on the man as the head of woman (1 Cor. 11:3) and as the wife being in subjection to her husband (Eph. 5:22). If the man is the authority over the woman, and the husband is the authority over the wife (like Sarah, "who obeyed Abraham and called him her master," 1 Peter 3:6), to the extent that the husband believes it is his right to determine when and how he will have sex, and that sex is to satisfy only himself, then she is being treated with the same regard as property and not as a person. Unfortunately, these verses on the duty of a wife to submit to her husband are overly stressed by some men, and tragically, violate a basic hermeneutical principle of forming a doctrine on the entire teaching of the Bible rather than on a couple of verses. They incorrectly attempt to push their wives into submission. We all have our favorite parts of the Bible that we tend to emphasize. From my observation, the parts we emphasize are the ones that make us look good or have a pay-off for us.

The atonement of Christ becomes the pivotal point

between the Old Covenant and the New Covenant and becomes foundational for the teaching of the New. The New
Covenant validates the woman as a person equal with
man (Gal. 3:28). The New Covenant also supports the
egalitarian male-female relationship in the sexual relationship between husband and wife:

> The husband should fulfill his marital duty to his
> wife, and likewise the wife to her husband. The
> wife's body does not belong to her alone but also
> to her husband. In the same way, the husband's
> body does not belong to him alone but also to his
> wife. Do not deprive each other except by mutual
> consent and for a time, so that you may devote
> yourselves to prayer. Then come together again so
> that Satan will not tempt you because of your lack
> of self-control (1 Cor. 7:3-5, NIV).

This passage clearly speaks of the mutual sexual
bonding between husband and wife. The point is that the
wife has exactly the same right to the body of her husband as the husband does to his wife's body. There is not
the dominance of male over female but there is equality,
both have the same rights and *each one* is submissive to
the other. Here the woman is validated as a person on the
same level as man and not as a piece of property, and the
logical conclusion from an ethical perspective is that it is
wrong to regard and treat the woman as property for sexual use or any other reason. But what about the texts in
the New Covenant that teach the wife is to be submissive
to her husband? Are they not contrary to the egalitarian
male-female relationship?

Hierarchy and Function

Do not assume from the foregoing that hierarchy is
bad. We have only to look around us to know that in
many instances it is good. We are told to submit ourselves
to governmental authority (Rom. 13:1) and to leaders in
the church (Heb. 13:17) and of course to God (Rom. 12:1-
2). Without an authoritative hierarchy, our cities and na-

tions would be in anarchy, which from the Old Covenant seemed to be much worse than the most tyrannical of dictators. Because of our fallen nature we need authority in order for nations, cities, and families to function well. Submission by anyone in a hierarchical chain of command, however, in no way implies inequality or inferiority.

Paul, in writing to the Corinthians seems to set forth a hierarchical chain of command when he says: "But I would have you know, that the head of every man is Christ; and the head of the woman is man; and the head of Christ is God" (1 Cor. 11:3). W.E. Vine says that the Greek word "KEPHALE" speaks of "the authority or direction of God in relation to Christ, of Christ in relation to believing men, of the husband in relation to the wife." If we look closely at this passage we note something a bit strange in this order. We see Christ in this chain of command under God. If this chain of command implied inferiority it would devastate the biblical doctrine of the deity of Jesus Christ who, the Scriptures teach in numerous places, is equal in power and glory to God. Christ is equal with God, but if we look at the plan of redemption, Christ submitted Himself. He was not forced to submit, but submitted Himself for a functional purpose, to make the plan of salvation work. Without the submission of Himself there would have been no redemption. "Subordination does not mean inferiority. The sexes are equal mentally, morally, and spiritually" (*The Complete Biblical Library*).

If we carry this thought over into the husband-wife relationship, it makes sense. Paul, writing about the submission of the wife to the husband, said: "Wives, submit yourselves unto your own husbands as unto the Lord. For the husband is the head (KEPHALE) of the wife, even as Christ is the head of the church: and he is the Saviour of the body" (Eph. 5:22-23). *The Complete Biblical Library* uses the verb "submit" in the middle voice, which means that it is reflexive action, which in turn means that it is something the wife does voluntarily. The husband cannot force his wife to submit because only she can choose to do so in order to enable the marriage to function well. The middle voice is also used in Colossians 3:18, Titus 2:5, and 1 Peter 3:1, 5.

A functional marriage does not end with this role for the wife. It is further described by the role of the husband: "Husbands, love your wives, even as Christ also loved the church, and gave himself for it" (Eph. 5:25). Husbands would do well to memorize this verse and attend to this role, rather than trying to force their wives into submission and blame their wives for a failing marriage because they do not submit.

From this perspective, a functional marriage, then, is one in balance. One side of the scale has the wife submitting herself for a functional reason to make the marriage work, and the other side of the scale has a husband who loves his wife the way Christ loved the church and gave Himself for it. Does this destroy the egalitarian relationship? No, it does not, because at times a husband is as well to be submissive to his wife: "Submitting yourselves one to another in the fear of God" (Eph. 5:21). A wife also is to love her husband: older women should teach the younger women to love their husbands (Titus 2:4).

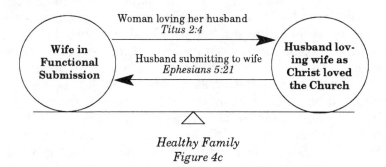

Healthy Family
Figure 4c

We are all in a hierarchy somewhere, and the context will determine which way the submission should go. In the context of the churches that I have pastored, my wife submits herself to me, but when I do group work in the hospital where she is the clinical director, then I submit myself to her. In this way, the church functions well, the hospital functions well, and the home functions...pretty well (neither of us have this down perfectly, yet).

Equal but Unique

Equal standing before God is not to deny male-female differences, which are many. Peter brings out both the equality and uniqueness of males and females.

> Husbands, in the same way be considerate as you live with your wives, and treat them with respect as the weaker partner (uniqueness) and as heirs with you (equality, marriage is a partnership) of the gracious gift of life, so that nothing will hinder your prayers (1 Peter 3:7, NIV).

Weaker refers to physical strength. Generally, males are physically stronger than females. Because of that difference, the husband's responsibility is to be considerate of his wife and assume the role of not only companion but protector. The word "considerate" in the Greek language has the idea of value and esteem. As Solomon said, "He who finds a wife finds a good thing" (Prov. 18:22, NIV).

The thought is that the husband's responsibilities should be to highly value and esteem his wife. Out of this high sense of value for her, the husband then brings a high degree of care, understanding, concern, tenderness, gentleness, and love into the entire arena of marriage. Obviously, this is easier said than done! These virtues seem to be what women yearn for – to the degree that bonding will occur. In this type of relationship, the husband will not continually try to control or parent his wife. He will instead give her freedom to develop and grow in her uniqueness, and to become fulfilled as she discovers more of God's plan for her life.

It is important for men to understand that the qualities of gentleness, tenderness, kindness, and goodness are not indicators of weakness, as the world system may view them, but of strength. Some men may view them as weaknesses and as the opposite of being "macho." This deters them from fulfilling intimate bonding with their wives. These qualities are not the natural way of behavior, but are products by the work of God's Spirit within us.

In this considerate, gentle care for the weaker partner, the husband, however, retains clear boundaries and does not surrender his beliefs, values, opinions, and responsibilities in order to satiate her every whim. But he does not seek to impose his BVORs upon her and thereby make her after his own image. He continues to accept her as she is and encourages and facilitates her growth as he can. The husband also must learn the art of identifying his emotions and needs and clearly communicate these to his wife. Again, this is easier said then done. However, if a couple can grow in their skill of doing this, they will go a long way in diffusing anger and in preventing a deterioration of the relationship because of "stuffed" feelings and unresolved issues between them.

Summary

The relationship between the husband and wife is that unseen entity that resides in the home with them. It must be monitored, cared for, and nurtured, as one would a baby, if the relationship is to bring God glory and be a sweet-smelling savor of holy sacrifice to Him. The boundaries of a husband and a wife, their BVORs, give them self-definition and responsibilities. These are not to be violated by the other, but respected in love. The responsibilities in both the husband's and the wife's boundaries, according to Scripture, is to be kind, tenderhearted and forgiving to one another. Submission is a volitional act of the wife in order for the efficient functioning of the marriage, not due to inferiority. Christ, in His restoring of His kingdom, is restoring equal respect to the role of women, who once were but property. Honest communication and hearing each other's feelings and needs, again, is a key to the husband-wife bonding.

Reflective Questions

1. Have you established your boundaries – your self-identity as a husband or as a wife?

2. Are you committed to bringing God delight in your role as a husband or as a wife?

3. What ways express your bonding as a husband or as a wife?

Discussion Questions

1. What boundaries – beliefs, values, opinions, and responsibilities – does God set for the role of a husband? A wife?

2. What issues, in our decades, does Satan use to detract from the responsibility and privilege of a husband bonding to his wife? Of a wife bonding to her husband?

3. How does God's expressions of love to us parallel with the husband's love-expression to his wife? Why is it important for the wife to take responsibility in her role of functional submission?

Chapter Five

CHAPTER 5
The Mother Side of Parenting

Ah, my favorite topic: being a mother. As a little girl, I played house, planned my dollies' days, fixed their bottles, changed their "Betsey-Wetsy" diapers, taught them in play school, and dreamed of the day I'd be a real mother. Many hours were spent in creating a home for these babies. In the summer my mom and dad helped me by providing sheets in the backyard for tents that served as imaginary houses. In the fall I raked the leaves into the shape of rooms as I formed my imaginary leaf houses. In the winter, a real dollhouse became my very favorite Christmas gift. This fantasy time was preparing my energies to feather my nest as an adult. When the real thing came, it came with double blessing. Twin baby girls were born to us near the Easter season. The hospital nurse brought them to me wrapped snugly in white blankets, tied at their little chests with big yellow ribbons, and soft pink bunny ears above their heads – I mean, my fantasy was more than fulfilled. My hours of imaginative play had readied me for this event. Certainly, many women become nurturing mothers without all the anticipation that went into my play, but somewhere the child needs to have seen or experienced the nurturing, teaching, enjoying, and protecting that constitutes being an effective mother. My own daughters never took their dollies as seriously. Yet, the four of us, including their little brother, spent much time having fun, caring for, learning and loving together. This is the mother side of parenting – bonding, the caring for.

Many mothers can't stay at home with their children when they are young. Circumstances of single parenting may demand that the mother be the only breadwinner. A couple may need two incomes to survive, or the woman may be the professional while the father stays home for the mothering tasks. Sometimes, because of lack of any readiness and the emotional complications or injuries in the background of particular mothers, it may be in their best interest and that of their children, for her to maintain a job. These are the realities of our times. Still, in order for children to be emotionally healthy and prepared for adulthood, they need mothering. If it is at all feasible for a mother to stay home with her children when they are young, and for her to be available to them after school while they are growing up, it is an invaluable investment.

Such thinking, or values, may influence the schooling and career planning of a young woman. Our daughters, Heather and Jennifer, now young women, look back at their childhood with a mother available to them and want to have the opportunity to invest that same energy into their children. Consequently, they discuss and plan their careers around being able to be at home with their children, should God bless them with a family. This has taken quite a bit of flexibility on their part. A person never knows for sure even if they will marry, or if, indeed, there will be children. However, mothering is not as difficult as it may sound, if it is given the high priority it deserves. Both of our daughters completed their B. A. degrees before marriage. We taught them to be able to support themselves, regardless of whether they were to be married or not. We believe that some kind of vocational or career planning is important for women, as well as men, in our society and contributes to their self-esteem and autonomy. Jennifer and Heather achieved this by choosing to acquire teaching credentials. Jennifer is married to a youth pastor, teaches school, helps her husband in his ministry and in establishing their home. They both plan to continue more schooling, but work it around her being able to stay home, at least most of the time, with their future children. Heather, engaged also to a youth pastor, is in graduate school. She plans to establish her career in counseling, before she begins her family and gives them her first priority.

When the twins were born, we made a decision we would sell our new home, if keeping it meant my going out to work full time, then as a teacher. It was our first home, after living for years in apartments while Rod was going through seminary. At that time, Rod was just graduating, and his first annual salary was less than the projected hospital bill of a double birth. As it turned out, I was able to tutor part-time in the home, stay home with the children, and keep our house. We didn't have much money but we had time for each other and all the important acts of bonding.

We made memories of taking walks together, and showing our daughters the different textures of the world, rough trees, soft flowers, and hard sidewalks. I loved discovering the world through their eyes. We laughed at seeing them covered up with flour as we tried to roll out a pie. They gained an avid delight in reading from spending afternoons on the local library floor while I read to them, then going out for ice cream afterwards. Best of all, their hearts and mine became entwined forever during the nurturing hours of rocking and singing love songs to them.

When the twins were small, we would all crunch into the rocker (rockers are a must for children and parents). I would make up words, as I went along, of my great love for them. Their absolute favorite was a take-off to the melody of "More than the Greatest Love the World Has Ever Known." They and I can both remember them enthusiastically imploring me, "Mommie, sing the 'Great Mores' again." A few months ago, in a special moment, I sang it to Jenny again just before she was getting married – bonding. Our son's favorite and special request in the rocker was, "I Love You a Bushel and Peck." His teenage years now are a delight to his father and myself. I believe much of the ingredients of successful young people and happy relationships, later, are in early bonding with the parents. I have never regretted that investment or its returns – functional young adults, loving the Lord and ready to serve their next generation. Thus, one must first value the mother side of parenting, allot the time and energy to it, and make choices that will make it possible.

What Then Is at the Heart of the Mother Side of Parenting? How Do We Bond and Then Care?

While I encourage you to consider the value and necessary thinking to allow a mother to be at home for her children, children need the mother side of parenting from both parents. My husband, Rod, has wisely taught that all Christians, females and males included, need to incorporate the traits of a godly mother. Bonding skills may come more naturally for women, even partly because of their childhood play, but bonding is necessary from both parents. Conversely, mothers need the challenge to embrace the traits of a godly father setting clear, but flexible, boundaries. We can learn from each other's strengths while we maintain our own. Paul, clearly a man with strong masculine traits of leadership and boldness, unabashedly models this wisdom for us in 1 Thessalonians 2:7-8 and 19-20, NASV.

> But we proved to be gentle among you, just as a nursing mother tenderly cares for her own children. Having thus a fond affection for you, we were well-pleased to impart to you not only the gospel of God but also our own lives, because you had become very dear to us....For who is our hope or joy or crown of exultation? Is it not even you, in the presence of our Lord Jesus at His coming? For you are our glory and joy.

This man, who shook the world, compares his actions and heart to that of a mother. What, then, are the actions and heart of a mother that both mothers and all people can learn from in order to be all that God intended us to be.

Gentleness is Paul's first description of a mother heart. This is seen first in body language. How we connect with children and others with our eyes. Kind eye contact, and taking the time to look at the child when you speak to them, communicates their value to them. I used to have to bend over or stoop down to talk to my children. This was for the purpose of honoring them with the gentleness of understanding eye contact. They might also have been able to see the twinkle in my eye that said I was joking with them or loving them. My eyes may even have been used to make clear a boundary or training. The last of our children now requires a tilt of my head back to look up to his 6 foot 2 frame in order to make eye contact. Either way, gentleness means slowing down enough to look kindly at the person and speaking in a respectful and loving tone. Even discipline can be given with respect and by clearly connecting with them; it may break the mutual bondedness between you and your children if you look down at them or over their heads. Sarcasm or belittling is only getting down on an immature level that they might be on. In disciplining, we should give clear communication and express the boundaries of what we feel and what we need from the child.

Learning to touch gently may be more natural for the smaller hand of a woman, but children need it from both parents. It's great to "high five" and roughhouse with children, but somewhere they need to feel that gentle touch that communicates they are valuable and cherished – precious. I counsel several women in my practice who are pregnant. Interestingly enough, some indicate annoyance at the bulk that grows in front of them, grimacing at the pokes felt by the active baby developing in the womb. Others display a spirit of respect and joy for the little one's miraculous development, smiling at the ever-growing weight they carry in front of them and gently patting and soothing the unpredictable little one's internal movements. In the latter we see bonding beginning, stimulated by the component of gratefulness for the child and expressed in gentleness. The gentle touch, as referred to in chapter one, is a way of blessing the child, and should begin here, in the womb. With birth, skin-to-skin contact, stroking the face of a baby, touching the curls with admiration, handling the child carefully – all communicate that he/she is valuable, cherished, and precious to us. This is mothering, necessary until the children increasingly require less and less of mothering. They will carry it in their memories as secure adults, ready to gentle their children.

Gentleness is not something in our genes, it is a fruit of the Spirit that must be sought and learned. If you were not "gentled" when you were a child, it will be especially important for you to ask the Holy Spirit to fill you with His gentleness – that comes from a heart that truly has a love for others. Learn to pat gently. Watch how gentle people use their eyes, tone of voice and bodies, and learn how to express it. Your next generation can be one that is "gentled," and more able to pass it on to your grandchildren. Many times, when pressures slow down, and people become grandparents, they learn the art of "gentling" – speaking more kindly, taking the time to pull the child up on their lap and rocking them, decreasing their stress over schedules, and "spilled milk." Again, my wise husband would sometimes remind me, "Be a little more like a grandmother with our children," when he could see I was getting tense and perhaps too demanding of them. I remember being helped, as a young mother, by that visualization of a gentle grandmother handling a particular situation and it would slow down my youthful impatience.

Tender care and *fond affection* are terms Paul uses to describe his mother side of relating to the people he loved. He expresses a heart that is willing to give God's message to them, but also his life. He was committed to them and their well-being – a task of motherhood. I love his reason, "...because you had become very dear to us." He had bonded with them. Mothers, as well as fathers, need to bond, thereby letting the child become very dear to them. Sometimes that is difficult, especially if they have unconsciously expected the child to answer their emotional needs. This is enmeshed boundaries, due to the parents not having their own selves defined and their needs met.

Parents need to recognize that children come into the world with empty cups, with very little to give. The task of the parent is to fill that little cup up with love, self-respect, wisdom, and tools for facing the world without them. Mothers who have their children in order to fill their own empty emotional cup, end up siphoning off from the al-

ready unfilled cups of their children; this results in dysfunctional children. These needy children, in turn, have
children to fill up their empty cups, producing more dysfunctional children. This is clearly seen in the teenage
pregnancies, when the young person desires to have a
baby in order to decrease her loneliness or lack of fulfillment in life. That baby has very little to give. If the mother attempts to siphon off his/her unfilled cup, she will
most likely drain the resourceless child and end up even
more lonely. If children feel the dependence of the adults
on them, it often engenders guilt in them. This tends to
promote codependence when the children try to grow up
and individuate.

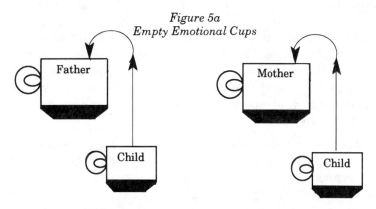

Figure 5a
Empty Emotional Cups

To break this generational transmission, a young
woman, or young man, must fill her or his emotional cup
up by building love relationships with God, friends, and
later their mate. They become people capable of bonding.
They work on developing their gifts or potential, building
their beliefs, values, opinions, and responsibilities, thus
becoming a boundaried people and well defined in who
they are. They, then, are ready to know what beliefs and
values they want to pass down to their offspring. Out of
their fullness, they pour into the emotional cups of their
children. This results in secure children who are getting
their emotional needs met, and less angry, less disp-
pointed, more fulfilled parents.

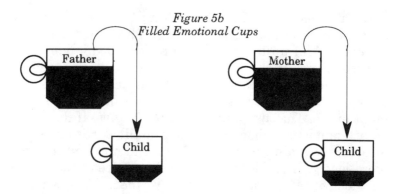

Figure 5b
Filled Emotional Cups

Not being able to be gentle or tender with one's children is often a sign of an empty cup in the parent. An example of this would be when the mother or father is consistently resentful of the child's normal interference in their lives. I heard a parent once say, "All that these kids do, is take, take, take!" There was probably a preconceived idea that the parent would be able to take emotional needs from the child. This obviously results in disappointment and anger. The parent's own emotional cup was probably empty.

Parents needs boundary skills also. This means that the parents must come to grips with what their values and responsibilities are to themselves, each other, and their children. Then they can kindly explain to the child how much they are able to give, be it of themselves or of their resources. Any immature person, without bonding and boundary skills, bearing children, is at great risk to face parenting with an empty cup. The parent is then limited in their ability to bond and give the gentleness and nurturing needed for a healthy child. A distraught older mother – after complaining about the traumas of drugs, scrapes with the law, and dysfunctionalism of her five grown offspring – recognized this empty cup principle and exclaimed, "Oh, no!, I see I had all those children for my needs!" Tragic hindsight.

Many times parents become defensive or offended when their children "talk back" to them or disobey them.

This will be a part of rearing children. If the parent is secure, having his/her emotional needs met by a healthy marriage, friends, and self-fulfillment, the parent will be less emotionally hurt by the child's lack of affirmation to him/her. The parent will then be more able to hear the spirit of the child and gently train him/her in the appropriate way to speak. This could include discipline, but not with an attitude of harshness or angry rejection of the child.

Ava, a mother of a 13-year-old son, exclaimed angrily, "He doesn't even speak respectfully to me! He's ungrateful and selfish!" She was incensed and wanted nothing to do with the awkward, lonely young boy. He truly needed much gentling and clear boundaries about what was acceptable and what was not. Instead, her energies were caught up in her disappointment in him not being what she needed for her empty cup.

Ava would need to take these steps to move into a more functional parenting:

1. Ava would need to assess and work on her own personal needs being met, rather than unconsciously expecting her son to meet them. This would be a way of maintaining an appropriate boundary with her son, rather than becoming enmeshed with him emotionally.

2. Ava would also need to clearly set the boundaries with her son as to what behavior she expects from him, with appropriate consequences if these boundaries are broken (the father side of parenting).

3. Then she would need to work on expressing the mother side of parenting. This includes watching for places to affirm him. We sometimes call this "catching him doing good" and praising him for it.

4. She would need to forgive him for not being all she dreamed of, or what she needed.

5. Then she could seek God to increase her feelings of fondness toward him. Her speech, attitude, body lan-

guage, touch, and eye contact are then her vehicles to convey his dearness to her.

6. She would need to look for more fun, nurturing times with him to increase the bonding – like taking him out for a sundae or a movie, or writing him little affirming notes.

The results would not only be more functional parenting, but very high chances of a more functional son – one who has experienced the healing of bonding and boundaries.

> We were willing to have imparted to you, not the gospel of God only (1 Thess. 2:8).

The mother side of parenting includes a love for the eternal spirit of the children.

Paul was concerned and had compassion that the Thessalonians know and understand the Gospel of God. As parents, our hearts must maintain a top priority of not only teaching the Gospel of God, but living it in front of them. If we are convinced that our children's lives are for the purpose of bringing pleasure to God and to further His kingdom of righteousness, peace, and joy (Rom. 14:17) then it is our responsibility to teach them the whole Gospel. Furthermore, we must be convinced as parents that because God loves them, they will be the happiest if they obey His precepts and laws. This takes our believing this, then our time and energy to impart to them this faith in God and to give them a purpose for living.

Deuteronomy 6:5-9 and 12:

> And thou shalt love the Lord thy God with all thine heart, and with all thy soul, and with all thy might. And these words, which I command thee this day, shall be in thine heart: and thou shalt teach them diligently unto thy children, and shalt talk of them when thou sittest in thine house, and when thou walkest by the way, and when thou liest down and when thou risest up. And thou shalt bind them upon thine hand, and they shall be as

frontlets between thine eyes (on your forehead). And thou shalt write them upon the posts of thy house, and on thy gates...then beware lest thou forget the Lord.

This is such a lofty admonition to all of us as parents. Not only are we to:

A. Get our own love relationship with God first, foremost and intimate, but

B. We are to know in our hearts His commands, then

C. We are to teach them to our children – regularly.

D. Last, we are to watch our own hearts again, lest we forget our God.

I have given much thought to these commands to parents. The following strategy is a practical plan for approaching the task of discipling our children. It reminds me of when I have been in committee meetings with a large, important task to accomplish. I get very frustrated when the discourse continues about all that needs to be done and how important it is to get it done, but I'm not hearing the essentials of accomplishing it. These are:

- Who is going to do it?
- When are we going to do it?
- Where is it going to get done?
- How are we going to do it?
- What exactly has to be done?

So, as for our job as parents to "impart the Gospel" and "teach diligently to your children," we have to ask ourselves the above questions.

Who Is Going to Do It?

While we are on the subject of mother-type love, it is evident that mothers have the responsibility to impart the Gospel and God's commandments. We've discussed that the mother is obligated to do what she can to arrange her life, schedule, energies, and enthusiasm around bond-

ing and sharing God's truths with her children. Specifics
will be discussed in the chapter on the father type love;
but truly, Father is the other main "Who" in this job description. He has the responsibility in his family, to teach
and model his beliefs and commitment to God. This may
seem like the obvious, but unless people see emphatically
what their responsibilities are in life, they tend to live by
the tyranny of the urgent. They do what screams the
loudest or is placed in front of them regularly, perhaps by
society. Examples are, everyone knows that their yard
must be kept trimmed and beautiful all the time, that the
cars have to be kept clean, that the house needs to be
company presentable, and even that the telephone should
be answered and people talked to whenever they call.
These are typical urgencies placed in front of us most of
the time. While these are important, the responsibility of
discipling our children is far more important, with future
lives at stake, here and in eternity. If playing, loving, and
teaching our children, generally, is not as urgent, then it
can be placed on a back burner while their growing days
pass into years, and, before we know it, the children are
young adults, already past the years of bonding and instruction. This can happen unless you state in your beliefs that your responsibility as a parent is to impart to
your children the Gospel and teach them God's commands, plus watch your own heart.

Without clarifying this responsibility of "who" is going
to do the job, we may not only procrastinate, but may unconsciously consider that the children are getting their
spiritual training and modeling from the church youth
group or a Christian school they attend. No, the "who" is
first the parents. We have to put training and modeling in
our priorities and plans.

When Are We Going to Do It?

I love the practicality of Deuteronomy 6 as it lists all
the possible "whens" for teaching God's commandments.
Moses must have had a hectic schedule like ours. He discusses using the moments. Talk to them when you are sit-

ting in your house, going places with them, when they go to bed, and when they get up; in other words, at every possible opportunity. Yes, he decided the "whos" were the parents and the above were the "whens" when they should go about it. I'd like to share with you some of our "whens" for imparting the Gospel and God's commands, so they may trigger for you some "whens" in your lifestyle and schedule.

"Sitting in your house:" The many hours logged in our house for discussions and for sharing our daily lives would be interesting to know. It seems to happen primarily after dinner, around the table. But our knowing that this is a "when" at our house allows us to lay aside other urgencies, like answering the telephone. It goes on an answering machine when we sit down for dinner, unless there is a real need for receiving a call. If the television had been allowed to run during this important "when" in the rearing years, it would have had the power to eliminate the family's delicate art of inquiring into each others' day and feelings. I find it impossible to compete with the high drama of cars going off cliffs or the fascination of punch lines on sit-coms, in full color, while I'm trying to ask my son what he is studying in his personal devotions. Television needs to be off during times you have specified as "when" times.

Discussing a T.V. presentation can provide another place for a "when" while sitting in your house. We have often discussed where the message in the media supports our family beliefs and where it is contrary to what we believe. This is crucial with the value system that is suggested through the message of television. Our kids know when to fast forward a video that may present an unexpected scene of immorality. Their action reflects our discussions of what we value, purity.

"When you lie down..." Certainly the tradition of praying with your children before they go to sleep is not only practical, but a prescribed "when" in Deuteronomy. Little children who want attention a little longer, or are

not anxious to go to sleep, present a perfect opportunity to spend some bonding, teaching, and praying time. Reading the Bible and other stories to them, talking to them about what is right and wrong, and worshiping with them as they prepare to complete their day, are not only precious memories, but is how their boundaries of beliefs and self-identity happen. Helping them set a special time to meet with God in daily devotions can be started at night, as you provide an easy translation of the Bible, a pen for underlining their favorite verses, a lamp and even extra pillows for them to relax in bed and read.

Particularly for our son, the good-night moments have always served as an important time to reinforce the many good choices he makes. I truly am grateful for his choices to live a godly life. Bedtime has always seemed like the perfect time to tell him of my gratefulness for the many fine things he does, or doesn't do. I still may pray with Chip, a senior in high school, thanking God that he is strong in character or expressing how I appreciated him being kind to a little child that day (he has a special gift with little children) or the way he took a discipline without resentment that day. Remember that gratefulness is a crucial component to positive bonding. We need to find moments to express the positive character traits we spot in our children. As we pray with our children we can set goals for them too. Such ideals to pray might be to always be honest in their school testing, to be fair and humble in their athletic events, and to be a good testimony among their friends. I know Chip and I are more bonded today because of the thousands of nights of sharing our hearts together, sometimes sleepily – but they built our relationship and his self-image.

"When you walk by the way..." When our girls were about 7, I taught them to run the sewing machine by making cloth covers for their Bibles. It was a momentous day when we pilgrimaged to the local fabric store, let them choose a half-yard of quilted fabric and matching binding trim, then came home to construct their own Bible covers. They both chose a bright green print with little red flowers on it. The coordinating trim was white, with red and green flowers. Their favorite part was the trimmed slim pocket on the front of it where they could keep a highlighter and pen for marking favorite Bible verses. There was a little pocket on the back too, to put their money in for tithing in Sunday School. They liked keeping this by their bed and using it for nightly devotions; and they were the "cat's meow" when they toted their own creation to Sunday School. This was an important "when," allowing us to pass down our values about God's Word to them.

Here is a "when" that is definitely relevant to having daughters: Our twins have always had long hair that requires a regular permanent. This demands several hours of one-on-one service every few months. This is a very special time for my daughters and me. We may discuss hairstyles and ways of enhancing their appearance, but as the hours go by, we always got into the ongoings of their lives. I came to anticipate this as a time where we would have not only some loving bonding, but a time to share values and beliefs. When you lovingly give to someone and want their best interest, it is a natural time to increase trust in communication. We might talk about their boyfriends, their testimonies at school, their relationships with girlfriends, or what each of us is learning from our devotions. The key is spotting these special times when communication can be meaningful, and protecting these moments from distractions, as we endeavor to use them as Moses told us to.

"When you rise up..." Maintaining regular family devotions where we open the Word together and learn "line upon line and precept upon precept" has been the most challenging "when" to establish. Through the years, we have met together, as school, sports, and job schedules changed, to discuss a time we could all gather for family devotions. Early morning has generally been best for us, before everyone goes their separate ways. Once we agreed upon the time, we had to make a commitment to each other to be there. We would agree upon a fair repercussion if one did not make it. Mercy and flexibility could be shown

if there was an emergency. The repercussion for coming five minutes late for morning devotions might be an extra chore. However, such rigidity was balanced with the respect for their different needs in the planning of the designated time. I recall one season when we even planned the time around allowing the girls to get their hair up in hot rollers, letting it "bake" during family devotions, then allotting enough time afterward for them to brush it out before hopping in the car for school. The mutual respect worked.

Where?

Now to designate likely spots. By far, the most sacred spot in our home is our kitchen table with five chairs. As I referred to in the previous section, we have spent countless hours around our table. A family of five recently shared with me that they only had three chairs (others had gotten broken), and so they usually ate on trays before their T.V. I thought, how sad to eliminate such a wonderful "when" and "where" for discipling their children and sharing BVORs.

Since we acknowledge our table as a "where," I take extra effort to keep candles there, not only for decor, but for burning. Something about glowing candles sets an atmosphere for lingering at the table, to relax and talk together. From time to time flowers or new place mats appear, mainly because this is our important "where" for devotions and we want to keep it as pleasant as possible to encourage our staying there.

We live 30 minutes by freeway from the Christian school that our children have attended for the past 14 years. That's a lot of hours racked up in the car with our children. Some years we have carpooled, but many times, it has been just our children or one of them being run out for a sporting event. This is a fabulous "where" to be alert for opportunities for sharing ideas and values with your child. I may purposely leave off my favorite radio station if I have an opportunity to engage my son in a meaningful conversation. One year we felt our "wheres" were a little limited with our son, so we refused the offer to carpool with another family, so that we could have that time to be available for a relationship with him. One year, when the schedule was right, it became a perfect opportunity for Rod and Chip to listen to Charles Swindoll. That doesn't mean that every ride was serious and heavy, but among the light, quiet or silly times, some opportunities were taken for creating a "where."

Since our son has become a teenager and is avid in sports, I recognize a "where" for him and me is at the local fast-food restaurants. He is always ready to eat after a game or practice, and I can connect with him there. His father and he enjoy sports together and bike riding. If Dad looks for the moments, he can find "wheres" to pass down his faith to him.

Shopping together has been a place where I can serve the children and discuss the statements we make by what we choose to wear. I've been known to carry back and forth 20 swimsuits for my daughters to try on in order to find that one which would make a decent statement, and serve to make them feel attractive. It's a team effort.

How?

We've inferred several "hows" in the previous discussions. Much depends on the ages of the children, but creativity and respect for the children's desires are paramount. When our children were between the ages of 2 to 16 or so, we tried to maintain some regularity in a "family night." When they were small, this consisted of some activity of fun together, then a family snack or treat. Often the content of the activities surrounded biblical teachings. Much of the time, especially as they got older, it was just for the purpose of fun and bonding together – or as our kids called it, "hanging out together." Here are some examples:

1. Once, with our 4-year-olds, we got long butcher paper and made an ongoing mural of the seven days of crea-

tion. They thought they were very special watching their crayon artwork go up around the kitchen walls, adding an additional scene of the sequential days of Creation each Friday night.

2. Another time, the children stood against a large piece of butcher paper and we drew around them, painted their features and clothes on the drawing, discussing with them the importance of using our looks for the Lord, and what attributes of beauty they were building inside of them.

3. We potted a two-foot-high branch in the kitchen, where we daily taped on nine different fruits of the Spirit, discussing their application in our home. I believe they can all still name the nine fruits of love, joy, peace, patience, kindness, goodness, faithfulness, gentleness, and self-control (Gal. 5:22-23).

4. As the children were a combination of junior high and grade school ages, we undertook the awesome feat of categorizing every verse in the book of Proverbs. I heard of the idea from Bill Gothard. Our children felt so proud of our work, they were sure it should have been published. We invested in two inexpensive paperback Bibles. Each morning as we met for family devotions before school, we cut out a single verse from this book of wisdom. We pasted it on to the papers we had titled with the basic topics in the book of Proverbs. (i.e., The Wise Man, The Foolish Man, Money, The Tongue, Relationships, etc.). A main reason the kids enjoyed the project was that everyone was involved and had power to make decisions. One youngster would cut out the verse, a second sibling would make the choice as to which category it belonged to, the third offspring would use a glue stick to adhere the tiny verse under the chosen category on the paper. We accrued a list of verses about each topic or concept. Each day jobs were rotated. The materials were kept on a large tray and pulled out from under the den couch early each morning. There we met on the floor to add

to our project and pray about what verse we had categorized. The children created a masterpiece of wisdom. I admit we didn't complete the book, we must have gone on vacation or something. But to this day, each of them value the wisdom in the Proverbs, and I learned a lot too! We all concluded we would rather be like the list of verses under "The Wise Man," than be like the description of verses under "The Foolish Man."

A Practical Point Is Time, Materials, and Schedules

Whatever we did had to have a planned starting and ending point. We had to round up the supplies and have them ready to quickly pull out. Everybody's schedules had to be respected. We held planning meetings and would all agree as to when we were having family devotions or family night. This may not be possible to start with older teens, but if children grow up with it, it is possible – especially if they have fun with it. For morning appointments, we would sometimes contract together, then Dad would put on an upbeat Christian tape, which would take about three minutes to resound clearly through the house. Anyone who did not get out to the designated spot for devotions by the time the taped song was over, was a purple pig with green polka dots. Purple pigs with green polka dots have an extra K. P. duty that week. You should have seen us all hustle to that morning music. This works out much better than fussing and yelling, "Come on!" It also gives you a chance to commend the children for their cooperation, good spirit, and just being wonderful kids.

Materials have to be gathered ahead of time and kept in a prime place for easy and quick use. Earlier under the section "when," I referred to the importance of the children feeling like their needs and feelings about time and schedules are considered. This is a team effort to grow spiritually.

I recall a supreme effort our youngest son made during a planning meeting about what we were going to do about family devotions one summer. Heather and Jennifer had summer jobs, being 18, and Chip, being 13, was the only one who could sleep in during the morning hours. We asked the question, "Do we think we could all grow, learn from each other and have better relationships in the home this summer if we committed to meet daily for family devotions?" Each one believed this idea was important since our frequently emphasized family goal has always been to "further God's kingdom of righteousness, peace, and joy" (Matt. 6:33 and Rom. 14:17). Because of Chip's evening sports schedule, the girls' work schedule, and our schedules, it appeared the only time this could happen was 7 a.m. Chip volunteered to set his alarm in order to rise with us, provided he would be allowed to plop back in bed afterwards. We all agreed; and we had few purple polka-dotted pigs even that summer.

An overall "how" is by building the bonding between you and your children. Children choose to imitate those they love and admire. The following section describes more of how to build that bonding and thus be more effective in passing down your values to them.

Safety is a key word to help build mother-side parenting (bonding) in your home.

Safety was addressed in Chapter 3. It needs to be incorporated here in developing a mother side of parenting also, because it is an important component of bonding, the tender side of parenting. Children need to have a safe place to be cherished and gentled in unconditional love. This love is not to be contingent on what they accomplish, but just for who they are, a precious little bundle of undeveloped energy. I like the phrase, "Loved not for being a human doing, but for being a human being." Chip recently had us listen to a song on his western station. He said, "You'll like this one, Mom." It was called, "Jesus and Mom Will Always Love Me." We laughed at it's twang, but he was right.

Do not compare one child to other children or siblings according to what they accomplish. This is a threatening environment. It threatens individual worth. When Bobby hears, "You just don't try as hard as your sister." This does not motivate him to try harder, but rather communicates to him that his home is not a safe place where he can confess his frustrations without condemnation, much less get wisdom from his parents on successful living. Possibly the areas that are being compared are not in his particular gift range.

Children need a home where there is safety to explore their own creativity and unique individuality.

Possibly, Bobby hasn't found areas that are in his ability range yet. The traditional school may not be a place where he will shine. If he is encouraged to explore areas that he likes, perhaps he will excel at something less traditional. Bobby may be destined to be a musician or a mechanic. An interesting study made a strong correlation between children attaining high creativity when the environment was the most kind. Do you suppose they felt safe to explore and attempt that for which they were a natural? Our homes need to observe the admonition in Proverbs 31:26. "She openeth her mouth with wisdom; and in her tongue is the law of kindness." This obviously needs to be applied to all family members, male and female.

The home needs to be a safe place to "brag on each other."

I could have said, verbally support each other. But, clearly we can't brag in public, lest others resent it. The home is a place where, because of our committed love to each other, we should feel free to build each other up and rejoice with each other's accomplishments. The parents can model this by speaking well of each other's work. "Your mother sure can cook!" or "Your daddy did such a beautiful job on the front yard, did you all see it?" If parents are filled with resentment for each other and withhold affirmations, how can we expect it to become a norm in the home?

A powerful exercise I give to parents who come to me for family therapy is: I ask the parents to write down a list of 20 character traits they would like for their children to have. This is agreed upon between the parents. This list might include anything from being "strong in faith" to being punctual, kind or dependable. The parents then need to keep this list posted somewhere in front of them – in their Bible, on their bedroom mirror, etc. The next assignment involves their watching for whenever they have any semblance of these traits in their children. The key is to recognize that trait and commend the child for it as soon as possible. For example, let's say "thoughtfulness" was on your list of desired character traits. If your son offered to help you carry in some of the groceries that day, you reinforce his trait of thoughtfulness by spotting it and telling him how much you appreciate him being a thoughtful person. Additionally, a very fruitful way of increasing bonding and building this concept into his self-image is to compliment him in front of his significant others, his family. Brag on him in the presence of those who love him. "You should have seen the thoughtfulness in our son today. He picked up the sacks of groceries and had them all in the house before I could even ask for help."

We have found the dinner table is an excellent place to reinforce positive traits in our children. Rod and I have decided that the table is a major "where"; thus we must not destroy this by getting caught up in excessive talk about table manners, negative discussions or critical discourse when the family is at the table. Obviously, parents would want to be careful about equalizing out among the children the amount of positive reinforcement or "bragging" comments. But if we are looking for those traits on our list, you can spot them somewhere in the most difficult child. And he/she may need it the most. As it has been said, we "get more bees with honey than with vinegar." I believe positive reinforcement of desired traits is ten times more effective than correction times which are also necessary.

Home needs to be a place where it is safe to be silly and playful with a family who enjoys you.

Humor is a marvelous bonding agent. And kids can be so funny. We need to laugh heartily at each other's jokes and stories. We even keep a place on the refrigerator door where anybody can magnet up a cartoon they enjoy and share it with the family. This provides some dinner-time laughs. People's attempts at being humorous need to be enjoyed. Once I presented a less-than-abundant dinner, a casserole and salad. Rod kept asking, "Is this all we are having?" When the two small dishes were scraped clean, all of us were first shocked, but then burst into laughter as Dad proceeded to eat the petunias from the centerpiece and, since that got such a roaring-laughter response, he took a bite out of one of the candles on the table. I got the message, and Dad made a funny memory; he sets a norm that humor is acceptable in our family. (I don't think he really swallowed the inedibles).

Every year when we vacation, our son surprises us by taking a mascot with us – a funny little stuffed animal. "Flam," a long-legged pink flamingo, joined us on several trips. His gangling legs could be seen hanging out of the pocket of Chip's carry-on luggage and in the center of our photos. We all think it's hilarious, and Chip is thereby affirmed as part of our family team. He recently went on a mission trip to France with a peer. When he came back, "Drool," a floppy-eared stuffed dog, was in the middle of all his photo travelog.

If the family environment is not safe, kids won't be creative.

Parents need to be safe people who will care about what's important to their children.

Basically, kids need to feel that you are on their team, again, a component of being bonded to your children. I hear so many instances where there is great conflict over what the children want and what the parents want.

These stand-offs need to be reserved, if necessary at all, for serious issues that will affect their welfare. Whether a daughter may wear blush in seventh grade or not, is not something over which to have World War III. But consider the importance to her, the competition with the other "beautiful girls, because they can wear blush," and consider her strong feelings surrounding your decision.

If we don't stretch our emotions to see what is important to our children and save the "No's" for the important issues, how can they feel we are on their team? Obviously there are boundaries to set, but they so need to see our concern for their sincere feelings. Appearances are important to the children of these generations. We can go shopping with them with a spirit of doing our best within our budget to help them look their greatest. I declare myself their servant when we go shopping, bringing different sizes to them in the dressing room and "nifty" outfits or accessories they might want to consider. What a different spirit I hear among parents and kids in adjacent dressing rooms. "You don't need that! You are so self-centered, and I'm not spending that kind of prices for something you won't even take care of." Or the kids, "Why can't I have this? If I can't have this, I don't want anything!" Somehow they aren't on the same team and the parents surely aren't looking for positive character traits to reaffirm, nor are the kids showing many.

When children know that you are trying your best to respect their taste and desires, and you have decided together to dress in a way that makes a statement for being a sharp, but godly person, then you can work together as a team to help them feel good about their physical presentation. I personally don't like this emphasis on labels on clothes. However, when you are in junior high, self-concept is pretty fragile and competition among peers pretty pressing. When our girls were that age, I did not work full time, and income was modest. Izod was the rage. The little crocodile on the T-shirts just made the outfit, according to the values of the kids. I know the twins felt I was on their team when they came home from school to find two of their new K-Mart T-shirts with Izod crocodiles sewn on the front. Their limited number of Izod shirts were all outgrown and budget called for lesser cost shirts, so why not transfer the desired little label and make their hearts happy? I trust Izod will forgive my plagiarism in the name of pleasing two little girls and trying to understand what would make them happy.

Last, children need to be able to trust their parents' moods and emotions. They need to be able to safely predict them as being nonabusive.

Mood swings are more of a problem for some than for others, but a safe home is one where predictability is possible. "Will Mom be cheerful this morning, or should I look out because sometimes she's a bear." I think it is important to make up our minds to be as pleasant as possible on the few times we regularly see our family. I figured that the main times my family sees me is when I am tired or worn out. I'm not particularly a morning person; so I have to decide that since this is our family time, I will plan to be cheery in the mornings. Similarly, evenings or mealtime when everyone gathers back together may also be a "worn out" time. I have to decide to be ready to relate positively to the family. Now that I work a heavy, emotionally pulling schedule with other families' problems, I sometimes have to take a little drive or even go around the block before I pull into my driveway and get my mind ready to be the mom or wife my family needs. It's a decision I make because I value my family relationships.

A major element that prohibits the predictability of parents' emotions and thereby decreases the safety feeling in the home is mind-altering drugs. When anything from diet pills that make us cross, to alcohol and other drugs are used in a home even occasionally, how can the children know who you are going to be? This has far-reaching effects and promotes insecurity and lack of trust far into their adult relationships. Adult Children of Alcoholics groups work on trying to build trust in adults who grew up in unpredictable homes. Our children deserve the same clear mind they innocently present to us. Their emotions may vacillate more because they have not developed their boundaries of self-identity – of knowing who they are and what they want out of life. We need to be as consistent and trustworthy as possible in our moods to build a safe and bonded feeling between us. The safety we find with our Heavenly Father is the same safety that we should give to our children. Psalm 91:2 speaks of our hope in God's safety. "I will say of the Lord, He is my refuge and my fortress; my God, in him will I trust!" We want to provide this trust for our children, making them feel safe and transferring this trust to God also.

Scripture tells us that our children will rise and call us blessed. Truly, as our job of mothering children is completed, there is no greater joy than receiving this blessing. I share this to encourage the many struggling and hardworking young mothers who have many priorities and decisions in their paths to completing their goal. May the song our Jennifer wrote and played for me with her guitar, on my birthday, inspire your continued efforts. This was right before her marriage.

My Mom Chose Me

Chorus
Musically gifted, talents galore;
Wanted by many, but granted to few;
Her titles were plenty, but one name she clung to:
Just three-e, three called her "Mom."

Verse One
When she had kids, Mom gave up a lot.
It'd be a long, long time
before I could see:
I wasn't all she could be.
Those days of discipline, years of instruction,
Her sayings still record within me.
They'll never leave, because I say them now.
Some would say she put her all into nothing,
Because one day I'd have to walk away;
She was "just" Mom and so proud to be
So proud to be.

(Repeat Chorus)

Verse Two
She served with pride,
and made a happy home;
Put her life on hold, so she could be with me.
She cared so much for me.

She chose her family, to raise her children,
A choice many refuse to make.
My Mom chose me – it makes me so glad.
Mom was there to help me through life's problems;
She knew just when to hold my hand;
She brushed away my tears, and calmed all my fears –
She calmed all my fears.

(Repeat Chorus)

Verse Three
Mom taught me lots –
to walk and read and write;
She loved to learn and passed this love to me;
But she taught me so much more.
She spoke of wisdom, and taught discretion,
And valued the Way, the Truth and Light;
This was her God,
and she brought me to Him.
With one hand she held her baby child,
With the other she held God,
her friend and King;
She held His hand, and put my hand in His;
The greatest gift she could give.

(Repeat Chorus)
***

Summary

The mother side of love is well defined in 1 Thessalonians 2:7-8 by a strong Christian male saint, Paul. He expounds on the elements of the mother type of love. We must examine our homes to see if we, as both mother and father, are demonstrating this kind of heart to each other and our children. If we are, they will become our "joy and crown." We will become bonded and thereby meet deep emotional needs. Discipling our children is also part of the mother-type love, "imparting to them not only the gospel, but our lives." For this task, parents need to allow the energy and time from busy careers and urgent tyrannies. This important task needs a target of what values or character traits we are trying to pass down to our children. Then it requires the practical plans of who, when, where, and how this is going to be accomplished. Safety is the descriptive word needed in our homes. This results in our ability not only to trust each other, but our God.

Reflective Questions

1. Is the mother-type love being expressed by all members of our family, especially the parents?

2. Is our home a safe place for our family, especially our children, "a fort in which they can hide?"

3. What personality changes do I have to make to increase the safe feelings in our home?

Discussion Questions

1. Why is it important for the mother-type love to be the model in your home? What components make up the mother-type love, according to 1 Thess. 2:7-8?

2. What are the "who," "when," "where," "how," and "what" that make up your plan for "imparting to your children the gospel and your lives" or discipling them?

3. What areas of safety would you like to increase in your home?

Chapter Six

CHAPTER 6

Fatherhood: Modeling the Heavenly Father

Ye are witnesses, and God also, how holily and justly and unblameably we behaved ourselves among you that believe: as ye know how we exhorted and comforted and charged every one of you, as a father doth his children, that ye would walk worthy of God, who hath called you unto his kingdom and glory (1 Thess. 2:10-12).

Families, including Christian families, are not always happy and harmonious. We all struggle with problems in everyday living. How we cope and adjust to daily challenges depends to a large degree on how functional our family structure is. In a functional family, the father and the mother have established clear boundaries in relationship to their children. They have established a clear executive parental subsystem. In other words, the parents are clearly the parents and the children are clearly the children. The reverse, which does exist in some families, would add to the dysfunctionality of the family. In a Christian family, the executive parental subsystem is responsible to teach their children (Deut. 6:1-9). Paul emphasizes the importance of the father's role in teaching by referring to it as exhorting, comforting, and urging you to live lives worthy of God, who has called you into his kingdom and glory (1 Thess. 2:12). A father then, should be committed to developing the child's godliness. One way to do this is by modeling a godly and emotionally healthy lifestyle. That is what this chapter is about. The purpose is to encourage current and future fathers to see the importance of their roles as fathers and to take action accordingly toward developing godly children.

One day as I was driving down the road, listening to a radio program (I think it was "Focus on the Family" with James Dobson, 1992), I heard about an incident that took place in a Southern California men's prison that deeply impressed me and illustrated our sociological need for writing and seminars regarding the implications and cause of this incident. Hallmark Card Company, in a desire to advertise their products through a compassionate Mother's Day gesture, offered to supply a Mother's Day card free of charge to every prisoner who wanted one. Their plan was to make cards available in the prison and to post them for every prisoner who would write one to his mother. Uncertain of the response they would receive, Hallmark hauled several boxes of cards into the prison, thinking that they had enough. The response was overwhelming. Without exception, every prisoner stood in line for hours to take advantage of Hallmark's generous offer. Much to their dismay, the supply of cards was exhausted with only slightly over half of the prisoners receiving a card. Hallmark was sufficiently impressed to make the same offer for Father's Day. Anticipating a similar response, they stocked the prison with enough cards so every prisoner could send one to his father. The response on the part of the prisoners was astoundingly revelatory. *Not one* prisoner sent a greeting to his father.

Many hypotheses as to why this happened could be set forth and should be tested before premature conclusions are drawn. But for our purposes here, would it be fair to say that there was a breakdown in the relationship between these prisoners and their fathers or that they never had a father-son relationship? And isn't it significant that each of these men ended up in prison going against their parents' wishes and, in many cases, prayers of parents, grandparents, and other family members? I believe the answer to both questions is "yes." I have yet to see a mother or a mother and a father, even if the child is unwanted, hold their newborn and say: "You cute little thing, you. I hope you grow up to be a criminal." Generally, parents want their children to turn out good. When they don't there is often much disappointment and pain. Generally, Christian parents want their children to turn out to be godly and when they don't there is much disappointment and pain. In the context of the sanctity of marriage God's Word says: "Has not the Lord made them [husband and wife] one? In flesh and spirit they are his. And why one? Because he was seeking godly offspring" (Mal. 2:15, NIV). At least one purpose of marriage is to produce godly offspring. For the committed Christian couple, godly offspring are children whose "God is our God and whose values are our values." These children know and love God for who He is, hold His values, and worship and serve Him according to His Word. Producing godly children is not an impossible feat. In fact, I suggest to you that it is easier than you think, especially when fathers understand the importance of their role and know what their job description is.

The father's job description is to provide his children with a view of God that is as close to reality as possible.

In psychology we speak of a *parataxic distortion*. I.D. Yalom says, "A parataxic distortion occurs in an interpersonal situation when one person relates to another, not on the basis of the realistic attributes of the other, but wholly or chiefly on the basis of a personification existing chiefly in the former's own fantasy. [It] refers not only to the therapeutic but to all interpersonal relationships."

This may appear confusing, but let me clarify this concept and explain how this has tremendous significance for fathers. When our children have severe parataxic distortions in their interpersonal relationships with their Heavenly Father, they relate to God on the basis of a distorted perception caused chiefly by incorrect behavior and attitudes on the part of their earthly father, rather than on the basis of the realistic attributes of God. In other words, God is our Heavenly Father and our view of Him may be distorted because we transfer incorrect and ungodly attitudes and behavior of our earthly father onto our Heavenly Father. A father's job then, is to ensure that his attitudes and behavior that his children may transfer onto their Heavenly Father will give his children a correct understanding of the true nature of God. Obviously, it is impossible for a father to do this in totality, but through his own godliness and perception of God, he can do more than he thinks to give his children a more accurate view of God. The more a child perceives the true nature of God, His love, graciousness, and kindness, the more likely it is that he or she will want to relate to Him and adopt His values and joyously live for Him. A basic assumption I am making here is that the more we understand God's true nature, His "agape" love, His "phileo" love, His graciousness and compassion, the more we will want to relate to Him. Communicating the true nature of God by our fathering style, then, is the starting point in encouraging our children to relate more fully to Him.

Children with distorted views of God are not forever doomed to a poor interpersonal relationship with their Heavenly Father. To some degree all of us have some distortion toward God. Part of our growth is challenging our misconceptions of our Heavenly Father and replacing them with reality and relating to Him on that basis. That is a life-long process. Whatever our age, says Yalom, sources are available to challenge our distortions (or validate correct perceptions). Such sources include pastors, youth pastors, friends, small groups, good literature and, of course the most powerful, the Holy Spirit using the Word of God – the purest and most complete source on the true nature of God. Yalom suggests that self-disclosure helps modify parataxic distortions. This enables our misconceptions and distortions concerning the nature of God to be challenged and corrected. Correction is one of the functions of God's Word:

> All Scripture is given by inspiration of God, and is profitable for doctrine, for reproof, for correction, for instruction in righteousness: that the man of God may be perfect, thoroughly furnished unto all good works (2 Tim. 3:16-17).

In Matthew 7:9-11 we learn that our perception of our Heavenly Father is linked to our perception of our earthly father.

Or what man is there of you whom if his son ask bread, will he give him a stone? Or if he ask a fish, will he give him a serpent? If ye then, being evil, know how to give good gifts to your children, how much more shall your Father which is in heaven give good things to them that ask him!

In this instance we should transfer to our Heavenly Father the attribute of a good earthly father. If, on the other hand, we had an earthly father that gave us a big rock and a rattlesnake on our plate when we were hungry, the whole concept of father – heavenly or earthly – would be a very negative concept. What the father gave us would not satisfy us; instead, it would hurt us. Would we want to receive the gifts of this father or listen to such a one, let alone obey him or live for him? No, we would not. This would be a severe distortion of God based upon the actions and attitudes of the earthly father. As fathers we must understand that we are the major input in forming our childrens' perceptions of God.

Ed Piorek in his lecture, "The Father Loves You," dealing with the fatherhood of God, lists three father types that cause our children to have a distorted view of their Heavenly Father. These distortions sometimes repel our children from God and place them under undue hardship in their relationship to Him. All of us function to some degree in these categories. To be aware of them and what they are doing to our children should cause every father to determine that he will not adopt them as a general style of parenting. I summarize these three father types in the hope of providing helpful insight into our own parenting process. See if you recognize, to any degree, elements of these types of fathering in your parenting.

1. *The performance-oriented father.* This father gives love as a reward for performance in areas such as sports, academics, chores, musical, and other achievements. Who of us hasn't been somewhat embarrassed at

the Saturday morning soccer or baseball games, when a parent very vocally humiliates his child because he or she is not performing up to the parents' standards? This parent puts so much pressure on the child to perform by rewarding a good performance with love. If the child does not perform, he does not receive loving acceptance or affection. This father type is very common in our culture. For the child this produces a perception of his Heavenly Father as one who demands religious performance and if he does not perform well enough, the Father will withhold His love.

I have a very good friend, I shall call Mike, whose father is very performance oriented. Mike became a very good athlete and musician in order to win his father's love. He still has not done this. When Mike and his lovely wife, both wonderful Christians, began to attend our church, Mike was ready to become involved in many activities. He and his wife became involved in regular church attendance, Sunday and midweek, youth work, Sunday School work, music, boards, committees, church programs, and other activities. As a pastor I was thrilled to see such a wonderful couple so committed to the ministry of our church. As Mike and I developed a close friendship, it occurred to us both after some years that Mike was competing for his Heavenly Father's love. As Mike was growing up, his very performance-oriented father gave him the impression that he would withhold his love for Mike if Mike did not meet his standard. If Mike came home from school with anything less than an "A," even a "B," he would be disciplined. His father placed similar standards upon Mike in his athletics and musical achievements. Mike became a very excellent student; an excellent, all-around athlete; and an excellent musician because he was trying to earn his father's much-craved love by performing to his father's standard. Unfortunately, Mike could never meet his father's standard, and, therefore, never please his father. Consequently, he never received his father's acceptance or unconditional love. Mike transferred his relationship with his father to his Heavenly Father. When he showed up at our church and became overcommitted, he was competing for his Heavenly Father's love. He knew of his Heavenly Father's unconditional love for him, but his performance-oriented life to please his earthly Father was so deeply ingrained within him that he did not even realize he was attempting to relate to God the way he related to his father – trying to earn it by meeting an impossible standard.

Mike never became or performed what his father hoped he would. Today he is in his mid-30s and does not have a good relationship with his father. He acknowledged that because he was competing for his earthly father's love, he was competing for his Heavenly Father's love as well. As a result Mike must be careful to keep from becoming overcommitted in church activities to the detriment of his family life, in order to attempt to win his heavenly Father's approval. He recently learned that he cannot change his father, but with the help of others, he can challenge his own misconceptions of God, which he received from his father. Having done this, he has reduced his distortions and is eagerly and joyously serving our Heavenly Father in full-time Christian work. A father's responsibility then is to model God's unconditional love for his children and not give his love only as a reward for performance. This does not mean that we should not have standards for our children. But it does mean that a father's unconditional love for his children never wavers regardless of how far short of the standard our children may come.

2. *The passive father.* This father is not around home much and not there when he is home. He is nondemonstrative with his love and concern for his children. Fathers who travel constantly; or who are workaholics, alcoholics, or divorced and gone; or who are emotionally stoic and even though they are there physically, they are not there emotionally, could fit into this category. The resultant distorted perception the child has for his Heavenly Father is that He is distant, noninvolved, noncaring and nondemonstrative. Those children learn that if they have problems, perhaps with their homework, Dad will not help them. Even when Dad is home, he is involved in

his own things, business, hobbies, television, newspaper or whatever. When the child asks for help, the father communicates, in one way or another, "Don't bother me, I'm busy with my own things."

A child wonders if this kind of a Father would help in time of need. "Why pray to this kind of a God?" they ask. "After all, there are 5 1/2 billion people in the world. God's too busy with other things such as the famine in Africa or the war in Europe. He can't be interested in my little world. He's passive as far as I'm concerned. He just doesn't care. How can I trust Him with my life? He's not around when I need Him." They don't deny the existence of God but in no way are they going to seek to nurture their interpersonal relationship with Him or seek His plan for their lives. The child here, often has difficulty getting in touch with the Father's love because he has transferred the passivity of his earthly father to his Heavenly Father and in his mind has a distorted view of God. Doesn't this describe a great number of people today? A Father's responsibility is to communicate to his children God's caring concern about each detail of our lives by being active, caring, and involved with the details of his children's lives.

3. ***The punitive father.*** This father gives pain instead of love. Pain comes to some degree through some form of verbal, emotional, physical or sexual abuse. Because children love their father so much, they cannot understand the harm their father does. The resultant perception distortion of the Heavenly Father is that He is stern, harsh, not supportive, punitive, unforgiving, and unloving. God is seen as the One who is just waiting for us to make a mistake so He can punish us.

Jay, a 13-year-old teenager, was helping his father and his father's friend do routine maintenance of his father's car. Jay's task was to pour a quart of oil into the engine. Jay, being totally unfamiliar with cars, stood looking over the engine with all of its hoses, wires, and other

parts in a state of bewilderment, trying to figure out
where to pour the oil. He knew he must do it because his
father told him to, but he had no clue as to how to do it.
The father coming around from the back of the car saw
his son standing there in all of his confusion. His loud and
angry response had a deep and lasting impact upon his
son. "What's the matter, stupid, don't you know where to
put the oil?!" Then he angrily yanked the can of oil out of
his hand and proceeded to put the oil in himself. The father's friend witnessed this event. Needless to say, Jay
was greatly embarrassed, humiliated, and deeply hurt by
his father's harshness. (To this day, Jay is so grateful that
he didn't pour the oil in the radiator). This young man's
concept of God, over a period of time, became one of
harshness. God was ready to humiliate, punish, and hurt
him if he blew it, either by acting or not acting. He was
just waiting for the lightening to strike.   Many people
have this same distorted concept of God. He is just waiting for them to mess up so He can squash them. As you
can imagine, no one with a reasonably sound mind, let
alone a child, would want an interpersonal relationship
with such a God. If they did choose to relate, it would be a
relationship based on fear and anger. A Father's love,
gentleness, patience, and kindness (fruits of the Spirit –
Gal. 5:23) are very important in modeling for his children
the true nature of God and thereby encouraging his children to relate to God.

Let me list some suggestions on how to give your children a correct perception of their Heavenly Father that
will stimulate their desire to relate to Him and adopt His
values. These suggestions are relevant for not only parents, but for each of us who may be transferring onto God
distortions that we have received from our fathers. Some
of us who are now adults came from a dysfunctional home
and received distortions concerning God when we were
children. We have carried these distortions into adulthood, and these distortions hinder our walk with God.

1. A father must minimize parataxic distortions of
God by relating to his children in the same way Our Hea-

venly Father relates to His children. Our first task is to understand how our Heavenly Father relates to us as His children. This then, will become our model for relating with our children. God loves us with "agape" love (John 3:16, 1 John 4:7-18, Rom. 5:8) which means it is unconditional. There are no strings attached. We cannot earn it but only receive it. God loves us also with "phileo" love (John 16:27), which is His tender affection for us. He likes us and wants to be with us to enjoy our friendship at home, school or work. Understanding and experiencing this two-fold dimension of God's love and relating to our children in a similar way portrays a striking contrast to the performance-oriented, passive, and punitive fathers.

2. Fathers must minimize parataxic distortions of God by learning to give illustrations to their children, in real-life situations, of God's true nature. My family remembers the Sunday we had an illustration of God's mercy and grace that we will never forget. I had just finished a sermon on God's mercy (sparing us the punishment we deserve) and His grace (blessing us when we don't deserve). At the end of the service my daughter, Heather, around 8 years old at that time, was tearing around the auditorium. As she was about to run by me at full speed, I caught her attention and sternly told her to stop running in the auditorium. For a fraction of a second she looked into my eyes and considered what I had said, while deciding if she would obey me or not. She made the choice and with a defiant look took off running in direct disobedience. When I finally caught up with her I reminded her that such obvious disobedience had earned her a spanking and that when we got home I was going to administer one to her. While driving home I recalled the words of my own sermon and decided to use this life situation to teach about the true nature of God. At home I explained to her that mercy was sparing her what she deserved (punishment) and grace was giving her what she didn't deserve (blessing). I then bent over and had her mother spank me as hard as she could with a wooden spoon (even though she denies it, to this day I believe I detected a muffled, gleeful

laugh from my wife). I then took Heather in my arms and sat her on my lap and, while hugging her, explained mercy and grace in terms of Jesus taking our spanking for us and how our Heavenly Father can now heap upon us undeserved blessing. Heather was impressed. To this day 15 years later, she explains mercy and grace in terms of Jesus taking our spanking for us. From that point on, we had three children periodically asking for grace. Look for opportunities in life to teach your children the true nature of God. This reality will go a long way in modifying the parataxic distortions about God that the child may have.

3. Fathers must learn to minimize parataxic distortion of God in their children by understanding that the family is an open social system. In his lecture, Mark Stanton says a system is adaptive and from time to time must change. Our Heavenly Father does not always relate to His children in the same way throughout their lives. For instance, we learn to be trusted with things of greater value by being faithful with things of lesser value. A father must learn how to promote his children to areas of greater trust and thereby instill in them a capacity for even greater trust. Rules and regulations cannot always be the same. As trust grows, the rules and regulations must reflect that new trust. Our relationship with our children must also change in order to reflect that trust. Stanton also says, an axiom of communication is that "all communicational interchanges are either symmetrical or complementary, depending on whether they are based on equality or difference." While our children are young we relate to them on the basis of difference. We are in a one-up and one-down relationship. We dominate and they submit, hopefully. As they mature they progress toward a relationship based on equality and eventually, hopefully they become your best friends. Although the adjustment may be hard for parents, it is important to make it.

Inspired by this concept, I sat my twin daughters down after they turned 21 and officially gave them a promotion from inequality to equality. I told them that no longer was I going to relate to them in a one-up one-down relationship, but that I was going to try to relate to them as equals – as friends. "Gee, thanks Dad," they replied. (I'm not sure that they, nor I, understand fully what I did). The goal of good parenting is to move from high control and low responsibility to low control and high responsibility as the child matures. God's method of relating to us is not static but dynamic. He gives us promotions and rewards us with more trust and more responsibility. That is a dimension of His nature that we must model for our children.

4. Fathers must minimize parataxic distortion of God by learning how to resolve interpersonal conflict through validating the feelings of their children and by using "we" statements. A "we" statement, Stanton says further in his lecture, is "a declarative sentence that seeks to locate tendencies, patterns, problems, thoughts, feelings or other experiences in a relationship or a group rather than in a person." In conflict resolution and problem solving "you" statements are often accusatory and condemning of the individual. "We" statements locate problems in the relationship rather than in the individual. A father needs to realize that before God, both he and his children are in the same boat of imperfection, and by using "we" statements he communicates to his children that "we" have a problem here, not just that "you" have a problem. In resolving interpersonal conflict, even if the father is 90 percent right, he still must take responsibility for doing what he can to resolve "our" problem. In so doing, he validates the feelings of his children. When a child transfers this quality onto God, he will want to relate to His Heavenly Father because He is one with whom he can talk and share his deepest feelings without feeling accused or condemned.

When Heather was in college, part of her requirements in being a peer counselor for her dorm was to go on a "Walk About." This entailed going into the Yosemite Mountains with her team of training counselors for a week with only a backpack. The most demanding part of the training was a 24-hour isolation away from all sight or sound of humans. Here she was expected to remain totally alone, take care of food and shelter solely from her backpack, and spend time meditating with God. This ruggedness and aloneness was definitely a new experience for this petite Palm Springs-reared girl, with lots of support in her life.

She reports the following experience. "The day began beautifully, with all the vistas of nature and the majestic mountains. I chose a spot for my meditation, high on a large, flat rock above a low, recessive cave-like area. I felt safe there from any rodents or snakes that might want to be my companions. I sang to God and had a meaningful time in His Word. As nightfall began to creep around me, not only did the comforting sunshine disappear, but all kinds of noises and shadowy movements replaced it. Most troublesome of all, a cold wind came up and chilled me to the bone. Then the rain began. And I was raining teardrops too. I knew I had to come down off that unprotected open rock. I climbed down, the rain pelting on my shivering frame, and looked briefly at the low, recessed area beneath the once hospitable rock. I knew I had to seek shelter from the elements. OOOh, but what was in there? I crawled in, fearful of what I might encounter. Then my crying ceased as I wearily considered these thoughts. If my earthly father were here, I could trust him to keep me safe from harm. I then will lie down, as there is nothing else I can do, and trust my heavenly Father to protect me. He surely loves me as much as my earthly father. I pulled my wool stocking cap down over my ears, that my earthly father had bought me to keep all bugs out of my ears, lay down on the musty leaves, and fell fast asleep."

This is a picture of peace and trust from a positive parataxical transference to God from her experiences of trust in her earthly father. She suffered no anxiety attacks and was kept safe through the night. As parents we need to live relationships with our children where they feel they can trust us and that we love them, to help build their trust and love relationship with God, their heavenly Father.

Summary

By now I hope we have a clearer understanding of the importance of the father's role in developing godly children. By understanding how God relates to us in His two-fold love of "agape" and "phileo" and relating to your children in the same way, by practical ways, in everyday life, you will communicate the true nature of God to your children. Once they understand how great their Heavenly Father is they will not only want to relate to Him, they will want to adopt His values and live with Him and for Him. After all, who wouldn't?

Reflective Questions

1. How is the balance of both mother-type love (bonding) and father-type love (boundaries) being worked out in my home?

2. How defined are my own boundaries (Beliefs, Values, Opinions, and Responsibilities)? – so that I know what I want to pass on to my children.

3. Am I operating in any of the three given parataxical distortions (false modelings of the Heavenly Father)?

   • Performance Oriented

   • Passive

   • Punitive

   Do I need to repent and relearn?

Discussion Questions

1. How can mothers and fathers demonstrate the father-type love to their children according to 1 Thess. 2:10-12?

2. What are practical ways to build boundaries – self-identity in children?

3. How can I minimize a parataxical distortion of God for my children?

Chapter Seven

CHAPTER 7

God's Hopes and Expectations for Children

"He was seeking a godly offspring" (Mal. 2:15, NIV).

We are not only to teach our children God's laws and wondrous works, but we are to teach them to prepare themselves for teaching the next generations, even the ones "yet to be born."

If we, as guardians, know God's expectations for children, we can more clearly set out that target for them. Godliness is meant to be a generational transmission; something that is handed down to each generation for them to take and pass on to their generation; not that it can't be started in any first generation, it can. But it surely is God's plan for each generation to be responsible for preparing itself to pass down the baton of godliness and His teachings to the next generation. Many times this is done, not only to our own children, but to other next-generation children through influences in Sunday School, children's groups, and friendships. We must make this plan clear, to each generation, of their responsibility to pass on the baton of godliness and God's commands. It gives them a reason and vision for really grasping God's truths, not only for themselves, but well enough to be able to teach it to others. We have found this to be a very practical principle in rearing "preacher's kids." They log more hours in church than most adults; they hear the same preacher all of their growing-up years; and they surely hear the Gospel many times over. If they think every message is only for themselves; they could say, "Oh yeah, I've heard this one before." We have encouraged our children to get the truths first for themselves, then to internalize it well enough to be able to teach it themselves. We explain to them that they will be spiritual leaders and influencers some day, first among their peers and then as adults. Can they handle the Word of God skillfully? Like David,

So he fed (shepherded) them according to the integrity of his heart; and guided them by the skillfulness of his hands (Ps. 78:72).

Recently, I asked Chip, "Son, have you checked out Psalm 78 lately?" I explained a bit of the above to him, telling him I thought this chapter would really interest him and affect his future role. Later in the week, I asked him if he had read it yet. He had, so I continued with, "It's clear to me that God gave you the particular brain, looks, and personality He did in order to influence others for Christ and advance His kingdom – His righteousness, peace and joy." I believe Chip is choosing to buy into this vision for himself, thus affecting his motivation to learn God's Word and grow spiritually. I believe it is solidly based in Ephesians 2:10: "For we are His workmanship, created in Christ Jesus unto good works, which God hath before ordained that we should walk in them."

We have discussed the plan of "who, when, where, how, and what" for teaching God's testimonies to our children. Note in Psalm 78:4-8 God's teleological thinking (thinking ahead) in His plan of passing down His teachings.

We will not hide them from their children, shewing to the generation to come the praises of the Lord, and his strength, and his wonderful works that he hath done. For he established testimony in Jacob, and appointed a law in Israel, which he commanded our fathers, that they should make them known (teach) to their children: That the generation to come might know them, even the children which should be born; who should arise and declare them to their children: That they might set their hope in God, and not forget the works of God, but keep His commandments: And might not be as their fathers, a stubborn and rebellious generation; a generation that set not its heart aright, and whose spirit was not stedfast with God.

Faithfulness to their next generation is a character trait we need to teach and extol.

We can model this character trait to our children, when they see how much we compassionately care about the salvation and teachings to our generation and the priority we place on this in our lives. We then need to pray with them for their ministry and testimony to their generation and to the next. I often ask my children, "How is your testimony at school these days?" I believe they do have influence for the positive or negative and they need to see the power they hold. We encourage them to memorize Scripture and meditate on His Word that, again, they might handle it skillfully, first for themselves and then for others. Heather and Jennifer have thanked us for our motivating them to memorize Scripture as children. They explain how it has helped them powerfully in their ministry during college. Each of them were peer counselors in their dorms and needed all the wisdom they could recall for that strategic position.

Various practical ways helped us present memorization as a priority to our children. The AWANAS children's club was a big influence and help to our children. It is an evening or Saturday program in many churches wherein children memorize up to 500 verses and gain the esteemed "Timothy Award." Also, we memorized verses as a family. Sometimes we took on the challenge of a whole chapter during a long car vacation – that was fun. For organization, we provided little booklets or notebooks (3 x 5 cards on spiral) for the children to keep by their bedside. I was thrilled to see these little notebooks propped up by each of the twin's bedside when I visited their college dorm. Probably the most influential is when we memorize His Word ourselves and share with them what verse we are working on. This might be in casual conversation, and just being open to share what God is teaching us through our memory verse meditation. It's a great way to fellowship with your kids from your heart. We, as adults, need the following wisdom too.

How can a young man keep his way pure? By
keeping it according to Thy word...Thy word I
have treasured in my heart, That I may not sin
against Thee (Ps. 119:9 and 11, ASV).

Children need to develop a repertoire of skills and tools to be successful in their future relationships and to serve God.

Relationship skills are a must, not only for their own
mental health because of their basic need to bond, but are
a must in order to help others. Children must learn the
essential skills of communicating effectively. Feeling and
expressing empathy is essential in order to be successful
when they enter adulthood.

These skills are meant to be learned with our family
of origin. Many times when I am working with teenagers
in my clinical practice, they have a perspective that when
they get on their own, all will be well with their friends or
marital partners. The truth of that dream is highly cor-
related to how successfully they were able to "get along
with" the people they grew up with in their homes – their
family of origin. They either learn the crucial skills of expressing their feelings, then problem-solving by asking for
what they need, or they act out their frustrations in rebellion in their marriages or adult relationships much
like they did when they were kids at home. If they had
temper tantrums instead of having communication skills
as a kid, they won't be very different as an adult. The results may just be more painful, i.e., divorce or loss of career. If they withdrew and pouted as a kid, growing up
isn't going to automatically change that destructive habit.
They have to practice facing and talking about their feelings and needs, instead of trying to manipulate. I often
stress to the kids I work with, it is for their best interest
to learn to cope with and communicate with their parents
as much as is feasible. *Growing up with a family is their
preparation and practice time for their future relationships. They need successful parental relationships
more than the parents do.* Granted, because of the acute

dysfunction of many parents as in addicted parents or abusive parents, this is very hard for their children and makes these children's practice years very limited. Young people still need to practice healthy communication patterns, rather than act out their frustrations, for their own sakes and their future.

Thus children need, for their own best interest, the tool of communication and empathy, hearing and caring for others' feelings. These are important tools in their preparation for serving God. Parents must take time to listen to children and teens express their thoughts and experiences. With two-family incomes and hectic schedules, "whens" must regularly be preserved for when we can listen to them. This is how we foster their communication skills. Many times we need to just listen, modeling the empathy skill they will need. Sitting down and giving them eye contact and our total attention is essential. This is how they will need to focus on their future significant relationships. I wonder how many hours I have spent with each of our daughters, one on one, after we have pulled in our driveway and finished a day of shopping. There we would sit in the car, listening and focusing on her feelings. This was especially true, during their concerns about boyfriends and mate-selection. Dinner was often late those nights.

Other times we need to guide our children through assessing their feelings about their situation and help them look for their alternatives, their needs, and their responsibility to solve problems. This gets increasingly challenging with teenagers. They, too, have busy schedules, even if it is just listening to their radio, in the privacy of their room. Nevertheless, we must set mutual times to talk together. These can be structured, like a family conference table, or sometimes we can borrow the kid's lingo and ask them if they can just "hang out" with us tonight. We might bike-hike to a fast-food place, have dinner and talk together, or go get yogurt or a video together. Do whatever you can do to "hang out" with your youth. They need to laugh with us, that they might learn to laugh easily as an adult and enjoy life. The word for obtaining talk-time with your teenagers is "available." I just can't be too busy myself as a parent, wherein I'm never available when my child is. How else can we pass down our BVORs to them?

Besides relational skills, stress to your children that they also need to acquire and develop some specific skills to serve God in the local body, the church. These skills are like putting tools in their belt and they can choose them according to their gifts. I have told our children of the frustrations I hear from middle-age people who finally have the time or desire to serve God in church, but don't really know what they could do. They feel they have never worked with children in groups, so they don't feel comfortable with the next generation. They haven't studied the Word, so teaching or leadership is stifled. Or they haven't ever done much with music or lay witnessing, so they feel intimidated to compete with other adults who have, and so on.

Again, we see the importance of this mind set to prepare oneself to tell the next generation. Music ability is a very helpful and valuable skill (tool) to have in one's belt, but the ability and plan for sticking with it should vary with different children and homes. We asked our children to place the specific tool of learning to play the piano in their belts. Then they could choose whatever other tools, or other instruments, they wanted to. Rod and I both play piano, so that helps that particular tool be a natural in our house. We actually made it a rule for our children to continue to study piano until they graduated from high school, just as they study math, literature or other requirements. Then, at that point, they could choose whether to continue or not. In order for our girls to stay in the sports, which they loved, they had to practice piano five hours a week. That was a great motivation for them, going through high school. They all three have a strong tool of music – specifically piano – in their belt today, which they now choose to use. Each of the girls continued to take advanced piano lessons in college their first two years. (Much to our delight!)

Many times they would have quit and been like the abundant testimonies of adults that took lessons a couple of years but can't play what they would like to today. So that plan worked for us.

Jennifer and Heather, now young adults, have chosen to pick up the guitar also. Jennifer wonders if we shouldn't have allowed her to drop piano sooner in order to pursue guitar. Maybe we should have. However, we set the principle that they could add any instrument they chose, as long as they kept up with the basic instrument of the piano. Jennifer uses both instruments now in working with teenagers in church and on mission trips with her youth-pastor husband. Both of the girls play piano for their personal worship and are able to accompany groups or individual singing. Because they can read music easily, they each taught bell choirs for the church's local Christmas program while they were in high school. They both chose, while in college, to add singing lessons to their tool belt, which they continue to use in choirs and solos. Jennifer continues to write music and lyrics that bless many. I'm sure there is more for them in music as opportunities arise. *This was a practical tool in their belt for serving the Lord and developing their own leadership skills.*

Chip, perhaps because he had their example or because he may be more innately gifted, has not had to be coerced to study piano. While he began lessons with me in third grade (a suggested time to begin children on piano), he made his own choice to work on improving his skills since about 9th grade. His friend, Ben, encouraged him by playing bass guitar with him. We, admittedly, were less rigid about his practice hours as he got in high school, because of all his sports activities. He might have lost his music skill at that time, but began to take an avid interest by himself and has been the church pianist for contemporary worship the past two years. He and his friends developed a Christian band, wherein he has played in schools, outdoor events, and churches. He, too, is pursuing guitar now, hoping to add another tool in his belt. He will be able to use music for advancing God's kingdom as an adult. I share this picture with you to encourage parents and children to see the far-reaching effects of having practical tools in their belts, with a desire to use them for God's kingdom.

I once watched a teenager sharing the Gospel and God's truths with a group of children at a Christian school assembly. He did this through his tool of ventriloquism. It was fascinating to watch how effectively this young person was able to maintain the children's attention while he told them jokes and then Bible stories through his puppet. We offered our children the gift of a manikin puppet if they would want to learn this skill. We discussed this in the context of our encouraging them to be preparing their belt of tools. They did not choose ventriloquism, but it helped them see the principle. Art is another tool Heather has chosen to work on. It is interesting to see how she uses it. Now we are delighted to receive her cards that she hand paints for us and her gifts of canvas creations. Chalk talks might be something she could yet pursue.

Learning to relate to, care for, and teach children is an invaluable skill for furthering the kingdom. If we provide experiences for our children to assist in Sunday School classes, help with Vacation Bible School or children's groups, their comfort zones are increased beyond their own age group. The skill of teaching others really increases this concept of their learning to pass down His truth to others.

Writing is another skill that can be nurtured, if this is something in which your child is interested. To watch them see their creations published is a real encouragement, if you can help them send in some of their work to children's magazines.

The gift of "helps" is not to be overlooked. If your child is sensitive to being aware of what needs to be done and can help people achieve it, he needs to see this as a real gift from God. This gift needs to be developed with joy. Not everyone is meant to be a leader; there must be helpers in order to get the job done. Knowing this is your innate gift helps you look for opportunities to develop and use it. Each child is uniquely made, and he, with his family, can ask God to anoint him with tools that fit his gifts. This will enhance his life and further God's kingdom – a win/win.

Children need to build a strong sense of their identity — boundary building.

"Even a child is known by his doings" (Prov. 20:11).

Morality (doing what they understand as right), in even a small child, is influenced by what kind of a child they consider themselves to be. "I am Mommy's big helper," so they go help Mommy. "I'm a nice little boy," so they don't kick their little friends. Rod is working with a 9-year-old little boy who says, "Yeah, I beat up other kids, and I like to do it." A child's image of himself influences what he does. Adults have a lot to do with forming that image. Chapter Five discussed the power of "catching them doing good" and appreciating the character traits they were demonstrating. It breaks my heart to hear a parent paint a negative image for their child, such as, "He is such a brat!" "She's hopeless!" The child generally believes that image and lives up to it.

We want, then, to build a positive self-image for them by how we treat them and what we say about or to them. Furthermore, it is considered an "adolescent developmental task" for them to build on this childhood bank of self-image and consciously develop their beliefs, values, opinions, and responsibilities. This is beginning to "take on adulthood." Their BVORS are the interior of what holds up their boundaries. A vast number of people, well into adulthood, have not established this adolescent-stage task, thereby allowing their boundaries to remain weak and leaving them with various symptoms of poor mental health, i.e., depression, addictions, anxieties, and psychosomatic illnesses (physical ills with emotional roots). One of the first things I tell teenagers who come into my office for therapy, is: "You're here at just the perfect time, for you're the age when you figure out who you are!"

**In our interaction with teenagers,
we need to give them this vision of their task,
and do what we can to guide them
in developing their beliefs and values.**

Building their BVORS is not only about God, though that is primary; but about their life purpose, about school, about sports, about their country, about relationships, about life in general. This requires a lot of positive exposure, talk, good reading, inspirational modeling, and learning experiences. Their values are like a hierarchy of their beliefs: what they rate as more important; what they love, enjoy, commit to. Children or adolescents who are left continually with baby-sitters, or even adolescents who are left by themselves to do whatever they can find to occupy their time, pick up whatever beliefs and values they happen onto. The only platitudes they may hear about are, "get what you can out of life, even if it means using and abusing others, but survive."

The phrases still ring in my ears of beliefs and values my mother continually taught me. She worked outside the home and had not committed her life to the Lord during the rearing of her first two children. They suffered hardships growing up and in their marriages. When I came along later, she was determined to "hand raise" me. This meant staying home from work, recommiting herself to God, and spending much time being available to me. She taught me as "we sat in the house, when we walked by the way, when I lay down, and as I rose up" (paraphrase of Deut. 6:7). I clearly hear her teaching, "Character is what you do when nobody is watching." "Come out from among them and be separate and touch not the unclean thing." "Nancy, if everybody is going to hell, do you want to go along?" "Your clothing and appearance make a statement of who you are," and many, many more. Mom and Dad's enjoyment of life, barbecuing, outside games, valuing friends and family and the beautiful outdoors are examples of how they have influenced my beliefs and values. There were negative examples too, such as high tempers, that left me with the task of learning a different way to express my frustrations. Mom taught me an invaluable lesson from a song she used to sing to me. "You gotta accentuate the positive, eliminate the negative, and don't mess with Mr. In Between." She would amplify on this by encouraging me to copy her positive ways, and eliminate her negative ways; she was giving me permission to learn better ways in the areas with which she struggled. I tell my children the same concept – and yes, I sing the song to them .

Developing their opinions and feelings may sound vague, but either a person does this or they are unenthusiastic about life and easily swayed by whomever they are with.

That we henceforth be no longer children, tossed to and fro, and carried about with every wind of doctrine, by the sleight of men and cunning craftiness, whereby they lie in wait to deceive (Eph. 4:14).

Letting teens make daily choices that are within their abilities and within your parental guidelines, like what they would like to eat, wear or enjoy, and respecting their choices, are ways to help them develop their opinions and feelings. An adolescent must be taught to be respectful of others' opinions and feelings, lest they be intrusive, disobedient and cross others' boundaries. They also need to be able to access and communicate their own opinions. Many of the fads and their generation's unique choices of clothes and music are an attempt to separate from their parents and develop an individual opinion. They may look like they're just following their "herd," but it is their way of breaking enmeshment with the parents, a healthy drive. Often, the only way they have the strength to do this is to do what their peers are doing – to latch onto another support other than their parents. They are trying to detach from babyhood dependence on their parents, but may choose a poor group with whom to gain their new independence. We need to provide them healthy groups to connect to, such as a spiritual, but fun church youth group. They need this support to make this vital cutting of the umbilical cord with us as parents. Within perimeters of what is godly and safe, parents need to respect their youth's individuality, rather than make fun of or mock their choices.

Chip has chosen to like western music, something unique to what we have enjoyed. Actually, with all his recent emphasis on it, he has taught us the fun in the rhythm of it – his opinion. Adolescents don't need to become rebellious to become their own person – and we want to give them that message. As Chip is preparing to go away to college, we have told him, you won't need to rebel from our lifestyle to be your own person. We will support your individuation.

Last, children, especially adolescents, need to accrue their life responsibilities in order to build their identity and thus their boundaries.

These responsibilities basically lie within the realm of the "F.I.S.S.E.P. Wheel," as discussed in an earlier chapter. The F.I.S.S.E.P. Wheel, again, specifies the six areas of one's responsibilities: Financial, Intellectual, Social, Spiritual, Emotional, and Physical.

Adolescents must increasingly see their responsibility to handle finances, learning to allot their allowance for their needs and extras and learning to honor the Lord with the firstfruits. When they get their first job, they must practice the responsibility of a budget, learning to save for what they want. My heart has always been touched when I see our children write out a check to church for an amount like, $17.39. Obviously, their part-time paycheck that month had been $173.90. Additionally, they must gain the vision of taking the responsibility of planning a way for supporting themselves financially in this world. Teens who have long-range career plans and hopes of being responsible for themselves tend to make better choices and feel better about themselves. This is not only for boys; in our society, girls often marry later or need to help with the income to buy a home. At times women may need to support the family, during their husband's illness or schooling. Girls who build careers to support themselves avoid the destructive attitudes of grabbing any guy to support them or get married only to get out of their parents' house. Heather and Jennifer have remarked how many of their peers, even in college, do not have this goal to be able to support themselves. The result is they are looking dependently for a man, almost any man. They have thanked us for setting the goal before them to be autonomous and able to care for themselves financially, as needed. It has helped them feel good about themselves and keep marriage as a choice, not a compulsion for survival.

Intellectually, adolescents must eventually take on the responsibility for developing themselves. Parents will not always be there to push them, especially by college age. Meanwhile, we can encourage them to develop to their potential during their growing up years. We can encourage children and teens to study by providing them a place or desk with good lighting at which to study. Even if they don't always use it, they see your support and value for them to develop intellectually. They may need your help in looking for a trade school or college. Colleges may seem overwhelming in price, unless you help them talk to a school counselor about grants, loans, scholarships, and work-study plans. Many times you have to talk to the college they may be interested in, or several college admission offices, to discover what financial aid is available. We made a choice in early years to spend our money on a private Christian elementary and high school for our three children. We knew then, this would mean we would have no savings for their colleges. When the time came to send twins to college for four years, the expense looked near $100,000. This seemed impossible, so we registered at our local junior college, where tuition was much more modest.

Our children desired to attend a private Christian college, so we also visited different ones. Some were discouraging and some offered us a plan. We applied for state grants (which never need to be paid back). We calculated student loan possibilities, planned for a work-study (part-time jobs), and figured what we could do to help them. Within three days of their university opening, the plans were resolved, state aid came through, and we cancelled our junior college plans. We packed them up for Asuza Christian University in California. Four years later, we all agreed it was a great experience for them intellectually, socially, and spiritually. They each met their life mate there. We believe they needed support in their intellectual pursuits, and they took it and ran with it. This has greatly influenced who they are.

Social relationships are of utmost importance to children and teens, not only for the fun and bonding but to help them strengthen their boundaries. They need people to whom they learn to say yes and no. Certainly we want to guide them to healthy relationships, but we need to value their efforts to make friends, and support them. One way to support children in the awesome task of reaching out beyond their parents and siblings is to have parties and invite friends over. Talking on the phone can be an invaluable way of learning to express themselves. Dating is an important way of becoming comfortable in the presence of the opposite sex and is an valuable part of mate selection and exclusion. The latter I do not recommend, though, until at least 16. The reason being that 14- and 15-year-olds typically have not developed enough of their beliefs and values to have safe boundaries to be ready to date. Some do not know what they believe about friendships and morality then, but it is almost impossible before that age. With the push of hormones and peer pressure, they need to be prepared to state clearly what they believe about boy-girl relationships before they are in the middle of them. This, again, takes time and teaching to help them develop a philosophy. We have encouraged our teens to thank God for the friendships He allows them and as a thanksgiving offering to leave them better than they found them; leaving their dates an example of a kind and godly dating relationship. I shared this concept in a women's therapy group recently and a 35-year-old mother of three children, divorced from abandonment, and dating again, came up to me and marveled that she had never considered that attitude about dating and how this was going to transform her relationships. This attitude definitely sets boundaries with current philosophies of dating for using and abusing.

Spiritually, each child and adolescent has the responsibility to maintain a personal relationship with Jesus Christ. He promises to guide them and be their Shepherd if they will abide in Him. This is their personal responsibility. Second generation Christians may have the pitfall of thinking they are all right because of the traditions of their Christian home. They may enjoy a cultural Christianity, only to find that will not carry them through life, much less eternity. They need to be warned of their personal responsibility to know Christ and the power of His resurrection – to personally love Him.

Emotionally, teens have to take on the responsibility of handling the curves that life throws them and, again, to use their family of origin as practice relationships for successfully communicating and loving. They need to learn skills like forgiving their parents and siblings, and expressing their feelings instead of stuffing them in only to come out in ugly passive-aggressive behaviors. Trust is a major aspect of being emotionally sound. One needs to trust that which is trustworthy. God is always trustworthy and is a fortress and a refuge.

"I will say of the Lord, He is my refuge and my fortress: my God in him will I trust" (Ps. 91:2). Many parents can be trustworthy as well as good friends, but none are perfect in all their ways. Teens need to seek out trustworthy relationships, maintaining their boundaries where they are untrustworthy.

Physically, the last part of the F.I.S.S.E.P. Wheel. Without adolescents taking responsibility for their physical well being, much of their life will be in destruction. For years we may have told them how to take care of themselves, but they need to realize that it must become their job as they increasingly near adulthood.

What they eat and how healthy it is becomes their choice. The best plan we can do for the hopes of their making healthy choices on their own, is to model to them what we hope they will do. (I could have gone all day without saying that, huh?)

> ...encourage, the young men to be self-controlled.
> In everything set them an example by doing what
> is good (Titus: 2:6-7, NIV).

I came into our marriage with a love for vegetables, because of my parents' delight in backyard gardens and all the fun memories we had in harvesting the latest fresh vegetables of ripe tomatoes or cucumbers or cooking the first big batch of new green beans. We truly got all excited about those momentous meals. That was a healthy modeling, and copy it I did. However, we also always enjoyed butter – on everything – and gravies and desserts. So when I got on my own, and began planning meals for my trim young husband, I took these values into my marriage too – and put 20 pounds on the dear man the first year. He still fights to keep taking those off. We have tried harder to model better eating habits for our children. Especially as we mature, neither one of us can handle the high fats and sugars without the price to pay – loss of trimness, agility, and health. We do better because we try, although we surely don't attain idealism. I've never convinced Rod totally of the joy of vegetables, but he started doing something very helpful to all of us a few years ago. He took up the art of juicing. Juicing vegetables and fruits for our breakfasts has made sure we all get the right vitamins and nutrients for our busy day, especially our "fast-food-on-the-way-home-from-sports" teenage son. We went to a juice seminar with Heather, and she ended up asking for a juicer for her college apartment. I must say, it pleased the heart of this mother to visit their apartment, open their refrigerator, and see it full of broccoli, carrots, lettuce, and fruits, instead of oreo cookies, candy bars, and pizza. Heather would pop a few carrots through the juicer in the morning before classes, add some other "goodies" just like her father did, and off she would go. Whatever food choices you make as a family, it is important for the children to begin to see their responsibility for themselves to eat a balanced diet, high on fiber, fruits, and vegetables, and low in fats and sugars. Rod bought each kid their own copy of *Love Hunger*, by Minirth and Meier. There is such a problem of eating disorders in our day, he wants them to see why they might make food a scapegoat for their frustrations.

As a typical family, we have tended to gain weight on our wonderful family vacations, except for lean-bean Chip. A couple of years ago we looked at our propensity for this while we planned our trip to the ocean. We agreed the four of us did not want to come back with additional baggage — on us. We problem-solved by deciding to eat out one time a day, a nice meal. Each midmorning we would take turns preparing a vegetable and fruit brunch for each other. What was most fun was: when we got to our condo, we took an adventurous trip to the grocery store, where all five of us were allowed the freedom to choose two favorite raw vegetables and two favorite fruits. (There was to be no cooking in this deal.) We ran around, each choosing interesting foods like mangos, strawberries, papayas, raw cabbage for cabbage steaks, carrots, etc. Whoever set out an array as a buffet for the rest of us, did it with flare and visual attractiveness. Later, after playing at the beach, we would bike out for dinner and a frozen yogurt. It was fun – and I think it might be hard to forget as our children plan their adult vacations and menus.

Because God teaches us that our body is His temple (2 Cor. 6:16), we need to pass on to our children the value of exercise in order to keep their bodies healthy and energetic. We talk to our own children about acquiring some sport skills that are not only team oriented, but ones they can continue their whole lives. Tennis, jogging, walking, swimming, and biking are a few we enjoy as a family. Because Rod and I sit all day in our jobs, we need to move in the evenings, if we're not too worn out. We do little things like parking the car a mile or so away from the movies, and walking the rest of the way and back. Heather and her fiance were visiting recently, and we all thought it was fun to "hoof it" together to the movies in the pleasant evening air. Granted we're Californians, with all year open to outdoor recreation, but each area of the country presents its own possibilities, including membership to a health gym.

Young people need to take on the responsibility of giving their bodies enough rest. Because Chip is leaving for college this fall, we were concerned about helping him see the importance of proper rest and thereby form a reasonable bedtime with his new freedom in a dorm. Near the beginning of his senior year in high school, Rod gave him a promotion. This promotion was his freedom to choose whenever he desired to go to bed. Previously, we had encouraged him to "hit the hay" by 9:30 or 10:00, especially during sports, unless he really had a demanding assignment. We have always discouraged television on school nights, with the exception of a treat or occasionally if all the homework and music was taken care of. (I would rather they call a friend and develop social skills or enjoy the art of pleasure reading than vigilantly watch T.V. every free moment.) The interesting result of Chip's promotion is, we are often saying, "Are you going to bed already?" as he chooses to head off to bed at a reasonable time. We want him to see the balance of work, play, and rest.

Sexuality is a big physical responsibility for adolescents. They have to harness it. In a time when sex can be lethal, we cannot mince words to explain to them how to harness it and take physical responsibility for it. Do not wait for your children to ask the questions; tell them clearly of the strong energy in them, placed by God, for marital union and procreation. They need not be naive by placing themselves in situations where they minimize the sexual drive in them, but should respect it and "flee youthful lusts" or as the *Living Bible* puts it, "Run from sex sin" (1 Cor. 6:18). As the text continues, this is the sin against your own body. Our communication to them and their seeing their responsibility is so important that I am planning another whole book on this topic. The same boundary setting of knowing their beliefs and values gives them the strength to "Say No to Drugs" and alcohol...and sex outside marriage. All this is about knowing who you are and being practical to not get in situations that cause you to forget, thereby letting others cross your boundaries.

> For the grace of God that brings salvation has appeared to all men. It teaches us to say "No" to ungodliness and worldly passions, and to live self-controlled, upright and godly lives in this present age (Titus 2:11-12, NIV).

Children need to move from a dependent position to a position of autonomy.

The foregoing discussion of adolescents building their BVORS and particularly taking on their responsibilities, are a preparation for the goal of their becoming *autonomous*. Autonomy can be defined as being able to function on one's own successfully – like the parents trusting to put their young adult on "automatic pilot" and his handling his aircraft with skill. We're still there for love and guidance, but our maturing children have to eventually be in charge. *This needs to be a conscious goal of parenting.* Without it, we can unconsciously cripple our children to always need us, or to be enmeshed with us to answer our own emotional needs.

When Heather and Jennifer went off to college, we had an important talk with them. We painted them a picture of us all sitting on a buckboard seat with a team of energetic horses in front of us. We pointed out that we had been holding the reigns of those horses pretty tightly for the past 18 years, though we had been handing part of the reigns more and more to them the past few years.

Now, as they were going away on their own, we needed to make sure they knew we were handing both of the reigns to them. Because, if they did not realize their responsibility to take ahold, what would happen to the energetic horses, the forces in their lives? The reigns would fall down between the buckboard, and like in the graphic movies, the horses would run wild, upsetting the buckboard, possibly destroying the poor drivers. They, indeed, would need to hold and guide those horses and make the daily decisions. We'd still be in the buckboard, ready to be called upon if the forces get too strong or complicated for them. Now, with the twins getting married this year, we're not even in their buckboards. But we surely maintain our buckboard near theirs in life, with love and respect for their own skillful handling.

We have said it is for the children's best interest to experience bonding, first with their parents and then to attach to other groups and individuals in their journey toward autonomy. Here the local church is the safest place to begin their detaching of dependency on Mom and Dad. Ideally, it becomes a surrogate family between their family of origin and their own independent family, while the church can still play a vital role for them in guidance and structure.

Another piece of autonomy is for young people to learn the importance of coming under authority where it is appropriate. They must learn to balance obedience to authority with learning to take authority where they are responsible to do so. They live this out by exercising respect and obedience to their parents from the time they are young children. This is based on their being taught the value of giving honor to their parents and those in authority who are honorable.

> Children, obey your parents in the Lord: for this is right. Honour your father and mother; which is the first commandment with promise; that it may be well with thee and that thou mayest live long on the earth (Eph. 6:1-3).

So teaching your child to respect you is not only all right, it is in their best interest. Your basis needs to be because God tells you to, not whether or not you think you do a good enough job. How children treat their parents in regard to respect and authority sets the stage and preparation for how they respond to school, legal, social and God's authority. It's like concentric circles (having a common center), with respect and obedience to parents in the small inner circle. If children break through that circle, in the next concentric circle the school tries to teach it to them. If it fails, the next circle of relationships, with their need to be submissive to one another, is in a marriage. It reels and staggers, and if this fails, the larger and stronger circle would be the law. It may have harsh dealings for one who cannot come under authority. Finally, God is the all-encompassing circle of authority and our ultimate Lord. All must bow their knees before Him in heaven or hell.

Figure 7a
Circles of Authority

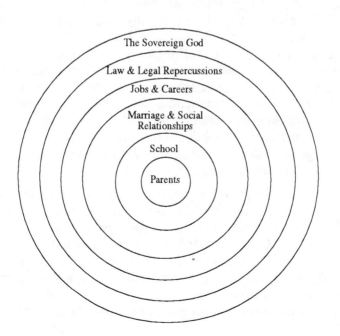

On psychological tests, how one deals with authority is considered an important aspect of his personality. Again, the young adult needs to have learned how to come under authority appropriately, and then how to maintain authority over his own responsibilities, temptations, and needs, increasingly as he or she matures.

Children need to recognize the wickedness of our times and to see their roles as "being separate, touching not the unclean thing," but set apart for holiness.

This begins by their monitoring what and who they allow their hearts to love. I truly believe young children can love God with all their heart, soul, and mind. I, personally, remember my sincere and devout love for God, at about 12. I had sinned by telling a lie on some neighborhood children, and I wanted my guilt and shame removed. I decided to try to punish myself by walking barefoot on some hot tar in the street. When I understood, from my mom, about the grace of God and my forgiveness by my faith in Christ Jesus, I was so in love with Jesus that I wanted to be a lady minister when I grew up. I vibrantly held church in my backyard for my little friends and told them about, "What a Friend We Have in Jesus." I even sang it with them. My father made me a pulpit out of a tree stump. The pews for the children were logs. Mother hung up drapes on the clothes line to give us some church walls. No adult's heart could have been more sincere. That devotion didn't change through the adolescent years as I committed my dating years to the Lord, and then my marriage. Children's love can be very fervent. We need to encourage them and take them seriously.

As children grow to love other people, and they have more freedom, they need to discern between safe and unsafe relationships. They must love people and look for places to serve, without taking on the "Messiah Complex" wherein they think they can save or change all friends. Obviously, with their boundaries not being completed, they are vulnerable to being pulled down by bad company. "Do not be deceived: Bad company corrupts good morals"

(1 Cor. 15:33, ASV). In other words, evil company corrupts good morals. The picture is like the dedicated young person standing on the table, and the worldly person being on the floor; who has the strongest leverage? Christian young people need other strong Christian young people to support them and bond to. They can then relate to the world with a loving and missionary spirit, rather than a dependent attitude of getting their needs met from them.

Choosing a life partner is not only for companionship and romantic joy, but is for serving God better than if we were single. Rod and I truly weighed this carefully during our courtship. It was a given that we were romantically enticed by each other; but our first love had already been given to God. Could we maintain this if we married? Could we consider that we could be more effective servants of our already proclaimed Lover and Lord by joining to one another as husband and wife? We have never regretted that careful soul search. Now, 27 years later in marriage, we are still called to our commitment to use our relationship and marriage to encourage each other in the Lord and to serve Him together. There have been moments where that consideration has brought tears as we have judged our relationship as not glorifying to God, but it has helped to put us back on track. Our children, our next generation, considered their mate selection with the same commitment to their first love, Christ. Thus, the effects on the generation yet unborn (their children) are at stake when a young person is dating.

"Be ye not unequally yoked together with unbelievers" (2 Cor. 6:14) brings to mind the picture of the field of life that must be plowed together. If we recall the illustration in Chapter Four of us being the oxen, we visualize how much better chance our children will have to complete effective plowing if they choose to yoke with equal oxen – those that have an equal love for Christ. Each ox, or each of the marital partners, are then less burdened and are happier. This, in turn, allows them a much greater opportunity to "yield a godly offspring," that God is looking for (Mal. 2:15). These are our Christian children.

Summary

Children need to seek holiness, not only for themselves, but to see their strategic position of being one who teaches others. They may very well pass the baton of commitment to God and His teachings to their own offspring. With that belief as adolescents they need to develop their own BVORS with well-defined boundaries, and also prepare themselves with a belt of tools by which they can serve to advance God's kingdom. A major place God planned for this to take place is in His local church. A goal for both parents and children is to slowly, but with planning and tenacity, move the child from a dependent position to one of autonomy. The major component of autonomy is taking on adult responsibility for their lives; financially, intellectually, socially, spiritually, emotionally, and physically. Maintaining respect for authority while they take on authority is maturity. Children and adolescents will need to see their calling to be separate and set apart for holiness. This is particularly paramount regarding the consideration of mate selection. They and their mate, as committed Christians loving God with all their hearts, souls, and minds, are not only to take delight in each other, but are to serve God better by being united than if they had remained single. This gives a greater possibility for continuing the generational transmission and promoting a godly offspring for which God is seeking. He cares about a generation yet unborn, that they would know Him.

Reflective Questions

1. Do we as parents see the overall picture of one generation's task of passing on the baton of commitment to
God to our children and preparing them to pass it on to
their next generation "that the generation to come
might know them, even the children which should be
born; who should arise and declare them to their children: that they might set their hope in God, and not
forget the works of God" (Ps. 78:6-7)?

2. How are we modeling our love for His Word and its
power in our lives?

3. How are we handling authority? Do we model obedience while we yet take authority over our responsibilities?

Discussion Questions

1. What plans are you now making or what plans can increase in your schedules to help your children value
and learn God's Word?

2. Discuss different ways you can see to help your children develop their gifts with the purpose of furthering
the kingdom.

3. Where and how are opportunities available to help
your child develop the task of building his identity –
his beliefs, values, opinions, and responsibilities?

Chapter Eight

CHAPTER 8

Bonding, Boundaries, and the Church

We have talked about necessary ingredients for developing and maintaining healthy families and have looked at God's expectations for the family; the importance of communication and managing anger; the biblical roles of husband, wife, and children; and proper parenting and role-modeling skills. As your family grows and matures, the cycle starts again with your grown children marrying and nurturing their own families – hopefully healthy families. Now we come to the final chapter which explains the importance of bonding and boundaries in the family of God – the "church family."

We were created with the need to have close interpersonal relationships – to bond – with both God and other humans. In fact, humankind's greatest need is the restoration of shattered relationships, primarily in a vertical direction to God and secondarily in a horizontal direction to humankind. At the fall of humankind we see first of all the shattering of the relationship between God and humankind. After Eve was tempted by the serpent we see the terrible consequences:

> And when the woman saw that the tree was good for food, and that it was pleasant to the eyes, and a tree to be desired to make one wise, she took of the fruit thereof, and did eat, and gave also unto her husband with her; and he did eat. And the eyes of them both were opened, and they knew that they were naked; and they sewed fig leaves together, and made themselves aprons. And they heard the voice of the Lord God walking in the garden in the cool of the day: and Adam and his wife hid themselves from the presence of the Lord God amongst the trees of the garden. And the Lord God called unto Adam, and said unto him, Where art thou? And he said, I heard thy voice in

the garden, and I was afraid, because I was naked; and I hid myself (Gen. 3:6-10).

After their sin, Adam and Eve hid from God among the trees in the garden. They tried to separate themselves from God because their sin broke their fellowship with God. At that point the curse of death came upon them, which is separation from God – the shattering of the God-humankind relationship.

But not only was there a shattering of the relationship in the vertical direction, there was as well the shattering of the relationship in the horizontal direction, between husband and wife and ultimately between all people. When God asked Adam and Eve if they had eaten the forbidden fruit, the couple's shattered relationship became evident.

And the man said, The woman whom thou gavest to be with me, she gave me of the tree, and I did eat. And the Lord God said unto the woman, What is this that thou hast done? And the woman said, The serpent beguiled me, and I did eat (Gen. 3:12-13).

What did Adam do when he was confronted by God? What all of us have done at one time or another. He refuses to take responsibility for his actions of eating the forbidden fruit and blames both God and Eve for what he has done. Notice how in verse 12 above he tries to avoid responsibility by pointing his finger at God and then Eve. "The woman whom thou gavest to be with me, she gave me of the tree, and I did eat." I imagine that his response had a heavy emphasis on the words "you" and "she" and a light emphasis on "I." Here is the first marital fight in all of history and by no means the last. Those of us who are married, could, no doubt, through the process of our imaginations, continue the script for this conflict. Eve's response might have been something like: "Well, if you would have been here instead of playing with those dumb animals maybe this whole thing would not have happened!" And Adam's response might have been...oh well, never mind. We all know how that scenario goes. From this point in history marital therapy became necessary as did lawyers, policepersons, referees, and umpires.

Also, from this point in history we see God as a people-seeking God, as He unveils His plan to repair the shattered relationships in both directions. As Adam and Eve attempted to hide from God, God called out to them "Where are you" (Gen. 3:9)? It would be false to assume that an infinite, omniscient God really did not know where they were. I understand His question to mean that at this point of His shattered relationship with humankind, out of a loving desire to fellowship with humankind, God immediately began the process of reconciling humankind to Himself.

The redemptive work of Jesus Christ has particularly affected the reconciliation of humanity to God and humanity to humanity. At the moment of Christ's death upon the cross "the veil of the temple was rent in twain from the top to the bottom" (Matt. 27:51). The curtain was the symbol of God's holiness – His unapproachableness by people. The fact that it was torn from the top to the bottom indicates that it was torn by God and not by fallen humanity and therefore signified that God is the One who opened up the way for us to be reconciled to Himself. Reconciliation of humankind to God is the heart of the Gospel message and of the Great Commission that Christ gave the church. Paul, in speaking of the affects of Christ's redemptive work, said:

> And all things are of God, who hath reconciled us to himself by Jesus Christ, and hath given to us the ministry of reconciliation; To wit, that God was in Christ, reconciling the world unto himself, not imputing their trespasses unto them; and hath committed unto us the word of reconciliation. Now then we are ambassadors for Christ, as though God did beseech you by us: we pray you in Christ's stead, be ye reconciled to God (2 Cor. 5:18-20).

Christ has made provision for all people, everywhere, to reestablish a vertical relationship with God that was shattered by the sin of Adam and Eve. This is life and health to the spiritual dimension of humankind. It also implies that evangelism (the ministry of reconciliation) should have a very prominent place in Christianity like revealed in Acts, the history of the early church. Even though reconciliation is far much more, in terms of this book we could call it *bonding with God.*

Paul speaks of the horizontal reconciliation when he speaks of the formation of the church as one body:

> For he is our peace, who hath made both one, and hath broken down the middle wall of partition between us; Having abolished in his flesh the enmity, even the law of commandments contained in ordinances; for to make in himself of twain one new man, do making peace; And that he might reconcile both unto God in one body by the cross, having slain the enmity thereby (Eph. 2: 14-16).

The "barrier" or the "dividing wall of hostility" is pictured by the wall in the temple court that separated the Gentiles from the Jews. These two groups were completely polarized with seemingly insurmountable enmity between them. If they could be reconciled, then any other two or more groups could be reconciled. Christ did exactly that. He reconciled, and continues to reconcile, not only the Jews and the Gentiles into one body, but people from every nation and of every color into that same body which is the church. That was the ultimate and the epitome of horizontal reconciliation. In so doing, He made possible and plausible the repairing of shattered relationships, even those with the most extreme differences. However, whenever people come together, even redeemed people, because each one is different and unique in some way and because none of us have shed our sin nature, relationships are often less than ideal. As an insightful poet penned:

> To dwell above with the saints we love, oh, that

will be glory, But to dwell below with the saints
we know, well, that's a different story.

Because of our differences there is always a potential
for disagreements, fights, conflict, and division. Appropriate bonding may be difficult in some circumstances and
we definitely need to establish clear boundaries. No doubt
this is why God has included much in His Word about our
unique place as a member of the body of Christ. We
should not, therefore, be jealous or envious of those who
have different spiritual gifts and talents than we do
(1 Cor. 11-13). Also, this is why God has included so much
in His Word concerning our interpersonal relationships
and the necessity and supremacy of love. The aspect of interpersonal relationships that we deal with in this book,
that becomes an important ingredient because of our differences and our calling into one body, is bonding and
boundaries.

Understanding the Pastor and Bonding

The pastor needs bonding with other people. The general rule is that if we do not bond to people, we bond to
things. Those things can become addictive and destructive. The pastor's spouse and family should not be
expected to meet all of the emotional needs of the pastor,
nor should the pastor be expected to meet all of the emotional needs of his or her spouse. Therefore pastors and
their spouses need other interpersonal relationships, in
addition to their family, in order to maintain emotional
and spiritual health. Some have said that these interpersonal relationships should not come from within the
pastor's flock because of a rule of thumb for leadership
that is used in the military that prohibits officers from
fraternizing with enlisted men. That rule is that "familiarity breeds contempt." This can be understood from a
militaristic leadership perspective. If an officer makes
friends with the enlisted men, then instead of receiving
the respect and instant obedience when he gives a command, the officer may be challenged. The formal hier-

archical relationship of leader-follower would be replaced with an informal egalitarian relationship, which would essentially eliminate authoritative command that is most essential in combat situations. For instance, if an officer had an egalitarian relationship with his men and he told them to attack the enemy or take the hill that the enemy was occupying, they may think twice about that since it would be dangerous, and they could be killed. The officer has lost command. Maybe the men would absolutely refuse to go because in their familiarity with the officer they have felt the freedom to question his authority to lead since they had replaced respect with contempt for him and his office.

Many pastors believe that this principle is necessary for effective pastoring and, therefore, have found pastoring to be an extremely lonely place because they do not interact with people in their congregation on an intimate interpersonal relationship basis. I understand that viewpoint and can think of situations in which my job as pastor was more difficult because I did enter into friendships with members of my congregation. When you know that your good friend is opposed to your position, it is harder to hold to convictions in decision-making. Preaching with conviction on certain topics when you have friends in the congregation with differing convictions is difficult. And it is difficult to be impartial or objective in leading without showing favoritism toward those whom you have come to love deeply and value their friendship. In these cases, familiarity could breed bondage in pastors' pulpit ministries and partiality in their leadership. Also, when a pastor enters into intimate interpersonal relationship, familiarity could breed contempt. One of the key ingredients of intimacy is transparency of who we are. Sometimes when church members see their pastor as human, with hang-ups, problems, questions, failures, and bad habits, they lose respect. The pastor is no longer on a pedestal. "He's human! He's just like we are! What right does he have to lead us?" In this case "respect" has given way to contempt. But not all church members are like this. There are a great many who will accept their pastor as he is, and who will not demand or even expect perfection. These will understand their pastor's humanness and will become a caring support for their pastor and his family throughout the crises of life and during the challenges of day-to-day living.

Intimate interpersonal relationships between pastors and their congregations pose some disadvantages, but the advantages seem to outweigh them. One of the New Testament themes is that we need each other just as each member of the human body needs every other member (1 Cor. 12). We were not designed by God to be loners and to fulfill God's plan for our lives with just "Jesus and me." We need other people. Our relationships with other people help us become what God wants us to become, and encourage us to become overcomers in regard to life. God has given every Christian spiritual gifts so that we can benefit one another (build up one another) and be built up by others. Pastors are no exception. They need to build up others but they also need to be built up by others. We see this illustrated in Moses' life.

> The Amalekites came and attacked the Israelites at Rephidim. Moses said to Joshua, "Choose some of our men and go out to fight the Amalekites. Tomorrow I will stand on top of the hill with the staff of God in my hands." So Joshua fought the Amalekites as Moses had ordered, and Moses, Aaron and Hur went to the top of the hill. As long as Moses held up his hands, the Israelites were winning, but whenever he lowered his hands, the Amalekites were winning. When Moses' hands grew tired, they took a stone and put it under him and he sat on it. Aaron and Hur held his hands up – one on one side, one on the other – so that his hands remained steady till sunset. So Joshua overcame the Amalekite army with the sword.... Moses built an altar and called it the Lord is my Banner. He said, "For hands were lifted up to the throne of the Lord" (Ex. 17: 8-13, 15-16, NIV).

As gifted and as tuned in to the miracles as Moses was, he needed Joshua to lead the army and Aaron and

Hur to pray with him. Joshua needed Moses, Aaron, and Hur to pray for him in order to be victorious, and Aaron and Hur needed Moses to lead them and Joshua and the army to protect them. None of these men were in simply a "God and me" relationship. When God called them to Himself, He called them into relationships with others. When God calls one to be a pastor, He is calling that one into intimate interpersonal relationship with others, and those others are most likely the ones in the immediate context of the ministry to which the pastor is called.

In the New Testament the life of Christ illustrates that He too needed intimate interpersonal relationships:

> Then Jesus went with his disciples to a place called Gethsemane, and he said to them, "Sit here while I go over there and pray." He took Peter and the two sons of Zebedee along with him, and he began to be sorrowful and troubled. Then he said to them, "My soul is overwhelmed with sorrow to the point of death. Stay here and keep watch with me." Going a little farther, he fell with his face to the ground and prayed, "My Father, if it is possible, may this cup be taken from me. Yet not as I will, but as you will" (Matt. 26:36-39, NIV).

In this account Jesus reveals the intimacy he had with Peter, James, and John. He shared his innermost feelings with these three, disclosing that He was sorrowful and troubled and that His "soul was overwhelmed with sorrow to the point of death." He needed and greatly desired these three closest friends he had in the world to support him and pray for him. How hurt, disappointed, and abandoned he must have felt when rather than pray for Him and give Him the needed support, they slept. Now let me ask you a question. If Moses, Joshua, and Jesus needed the prayer, care, and support of others in intimate interpersonal relationships, don't you? And what about your pastors – can they be expected to be the people of God they should be if they are living in isolation from the people to whom God has called them to minister? And will you allow your pastor to have close supportive friends from among your congregation even if you are not one of those close friends? Partiality you say? Then Jesus was partial when he chose Peter, James, and John to support Him; and Moses was partial when he chose Aaron and Hur to support him. Pastors and their families are human. Let them bond to other people so that in their humanness they can find what they so desperately need – supportive, caring, interpersonal relationships. But a pastor cannot bond to everyone, not even to many. Therefore, he must learn to set boundaries.

Understanding the Pastor and Boundaries

Pastors often find themselves in a lose/lose dilemma where no matter what they do they will receive negative repercussions. Does the new pastor endorse the replacement of the much-loved organist who has been the church organist for many years, but because of her age is having difficulty playing the organ and doesn't realize it? The pastor and others are aware of the organist's declining ability but also know that because she is much-loved and dependent upon the salary she receives, it would be judged as cruel to replace her. If the pastor acts, he is in trouble with some in the congregation. If he does not act, then he is in trouble with yet another group in his congregation. And if the pastor tries to leave the decision to the music committee, he is accused of not taking leadership. Anyway the music committee is looking to the pastor for direction. This is but one example of the myriad of lose/lose situations that pastors face. One of the challenges of pastoring is being creative enough to turn these potentially lose/lose situations into win/win situations. Sometimes pastors are able to do that. In fact many times they may be able to do that, but unfortunately inability to do that just one time is often enough to generate church conflict or to start a movement to remove the pastor.

What has this example to do with boundaries? You will recall from previous chapters that boundaries define who we are. In other words our beliefs, values, opinions,

and responsibilities define who we are. Pastors who are
not clear on these four areas can be easily manipulated
and influenced. We all need boundaries – those fences
that contain our beliefs, values, opinions, and responsibilities. In the above example, the pastor was clear
on his beliefs, values, opinions, and responsibilities. He
believed that worship of God is extremely important and
that good music is necessary for good worship. He greatly
values excellence in the worship service and his opinion is
that the current organist leaves the congregation tense
and embarrassed for the organist, and that her music is a
distraction from worship rather than a help. The pastor,
because of his office, has assumed responsibility for providing leadership in this situation. Therefore, if he is to be
himself he must maintain clear boundaries by clearly and
appropriately communicating his beliefs, values, opinions,
and carrying out his responsibilities. Congregations need
to support these beliefs, values, opinions, and responsibilities of the pastor without splitting him off as
worthless, incompetent, and bad. Pastors also need to
make the same concession to the members of their congregations.

Pastors who do not have clear boundaries (a clear
sense of self: of their BVORs) may appear to be very
teachable and adaptable, but may really be "yanked"
around by the beliefs, values, and opinions of others. A
pastor with a clear sense of self will be firm and appear,
perhaps, to be stubborn and unyielding, but will act and
speak in accordance with his clear sense of self. A pastor
needs to keep his boundaries. A chief way to do this is by
learning to say "no" to many of the expectations that people place upon pastors. People with high expectations for
pastors do not like to hear the word "no." However, if pastors cannot say "no," then their bonding to the congregation soon becomes bondage. The church members also
need to have the ability to say "no" to keep from being manipulated by forceful, strong, authoritarian leaders.

Our beliefs, values, opinions, and responsibilities
should not be thought of as static but dynamic. That is,

they are always in process of developing. Our sanctification could be defined in terms of our beliefs, values, and opinions as becoming more like Christ in His beliefs, values, and opinions. A renewed mind, or a mind in the renewing process, might be thought of as beliefs, values, opinions, and responsibilities that are conforming more and more to Scriptures. Interaction among staff and members, and among members themselves, help change who we are because through this interaction our beliefs, values, opinions, and responsibilities are shaped and clarified. Hopefully the results will be that each one is more Christlike. That, however, is not always the case.

The Family and the Church

Churches also have distinctive personalities because they have their own beliefs, values, opinions, and responsibilities (or mission defined by their programs). There is no perfect church. If there were, we would still judge it to be very imperfect if its beliefs, values, opinions, and responsibilities were different from ours. We generally select churches where their BVORs are as close as possible to ours although a true match is impossible. Therefore, when a church does something that is contrary to our BVORs, we tend to criticize it. As long as the church functions close to our BVORs we like it and tend to idealize it. An important function in the process of a family bonding to a church body is what we refer to as integration. Integration is the recognition that a church or a person is neither all good nor all bad, but some of each, and then accepting that church or person with both the good and bad. If we can't do this, then we tend to swing from one extreme of idealizing the church to that of criticizing the church and writing it off in totality. We must understand that there is both good and bad or strengths and weaknesses in every church just as there is in every person. If we cannot integrate the good and the bad with churches we become church hoppers. Church hoppers are always looking for the church with the perfect match to their BVORs. For a while they may think that they have found one, and they idealize that church. But when the church does something "bad" in the member's opinion, he or she swings to severe criticism of the church, rejects the church, then moves on to continue that quest for the perfect church.

Parents need to model integration to their children. No person is perfect. No church is perfect. When we find the church close to our BVORs, it is important that we accept the bad along with the good and continue to support and pray for the church. Attend the church with the children, financially support the church, and frequently express in the presence of your children how grateful you are for that church. This will enable the family to bond to the church in long-term commitment and will teach our children to value the church and give it a place in our daily lives. If parents split the church off, first idealize and then criticize and leave, they will fail to pass down to the next generation the value of the church. They quench the children's service to God.

Suggestions for Family Activities for Healthy Bonding and Boundaries

1. Teach and understand the beliefs, values, opinions, and responsibilities of your church. Most churches have a doctrinal statement with scriptural references. Take time daily to teach the doctrine, look up scriptural references and discuss what they mean. This is an excellent project for family devotions. Not only will this serve to acquaint the family with the beliefs of the church, but it also will familiarize the entire family with some of the fundamental doctrines of the faith since most doctrinal statements set forth the church's position in the major doctrinal areas.

Also acquaint the family with the church mission or purpose statement along with the programs of the church and look for ways for the family to support them. Another important, often overlooked but very valuable teaching aid, is the assortment of missionary letters that generally come to the church. Read the letters and pray for the missionaries. These letters will reinforce the church's BVORs as well as inform the family as to what is going on worldwide. These letters will also show how good doctrine is internalized and acted out as well as being intellectually understood. In doing this, children will develop a vision for how they can serve God in their generation.

2. Set a daily time for family devotions that disciple the children. Be creative and make them fun. They don't have to be long sessions, but be consistent. In the prayer time, pray for one another and for the church.

> Who is it he is trying to teach? To whom is he explaining his message? To children weaned from their milk, To those just taken from the breast? For it is Do and do, do and do, rule on rule, rule on rule; a little here, a little there (Isa. 28:9-10, NIV).

Parents should assume this responsibility for discipling their children. They should not relinquish this responsibility to the church or Christian school. These are adjunct institutions to help parents "train up a child in the way he should go."

3. Monitor the degree of commitment. Watch out for enmeshment. Sometimes families overcommit themselves to the activities and programs of the church to the point where there is no time together as a family. This would be bonding too much to a church (bondage) which is called enmeshment. Learn to set priorities and function by them. The most important priority is each family member's relationship to Jesus Christ. Second is each family member's commitment to one another. Third is the family's commitment to the church. Especially in very active churches there could be a tendency of the church's schedule to usurp the first two priorities. Pastors should be aware that overcommitted husbands, wives or families may mean that there are problems at home. Sometimes people use overcommitment to the church to avoid dealing with difficult or painful relationships or issues at home.

God promises us that if our number one priority is to "seek first His Kingdom and His righteousness," He will be faithful to meet all of our needs (Matt. 6:33). Among these needs in the lives of our children will be a passion for God, a love for people, and a respect for the church of Jesus Christ.

Reflective Questions

1. Evaluate your bonding between yourself and your God, your family and your church.

2. Have you considered the local church as God's vehicle for doing His work and purporting the Gospel?

3. Do you need to set more practical boundaries on the needs at the church in which you are involved, as opposed to the needs of your time with Christ or your family?

4. Are you able to accept the negatives along with the positives of your church?

Discussion Questions

1. What would healthy bonding to a church look like?

2. What legacy or attitudes toward the church do we want to leave our children?

3. What healthy boundaries (beliefs and values) do we need to consider concerning our relationship to the church?

Bibliography

Bibliography

Beattie, Melody. *Co-Dependent No More.* Center City, MN: Hazelden, 1987

Bilezikian, G. *Beyond Sex Roles.* Grand Rapids: Baker Book House, 1985.

Carder, Dave; Hendin, Earl; Townsend, John; Cloud, Henry; Browand, Alice. *Secrets of Your Family Tree.* Chicago, IL: Moody Press, 1991.

Christianson, Larry. *The Christian Family.* Minneapolis, MN: Bethany Fellowship, 1970.

Clary, M. "Out of Control." *The Los Angeles Times,* March 23, 1992.

Cloud, Henry. *Changes That Heal.* Grand Rapids, MI: Zondervan, 1992.

Complete Biblical Library. Springfield, Missouri: Complete Biblical Library, 1986.

Countryman, L. W. *Dirt, Greed, Sex.* Philadelphia: Fortress Press, 1988.

Curran, Dolores, *Traits of a Healthy Family.* New York: Ballantine Books,1983.

Dobson, James. "Focus on the Family" Radio Program. Colorado Springs, CO, Winter 1992.

Dobson, James. *Parenting Isn't for Cowards.* Minneappolis, MN: Grason, 1987.

Goldenberg, Irene; Goldenberg, Herbert. *Family Therapy, an Overview.* Second Edition. Monterey, CA: Brooks & Cole, 1985.

Hemfelt, Robert; Minirth, Frank; Meier, Paul. *Love is a Choice.* Nashville, TN: Thomas Nelson, 1989.

Mellody, Pia. *Facing Codependence.* Grand Rapids, MI: Harper & Row, 1989.

Piorek, E. Lecture: "The Father Loves You." Anaheim, CA, 1989.

Smalley, Gary; Trent, John. *The Blessing.* Nashville, TN: Thomas Nelson, 1986.

Stanton, M. Class Lecture: "Communication Theory in Group Process." San Bernardino, CA.

Stoop, David; Masteller, James. *Forgiving Our Parents Forgiving Ourselves.* Ann Arbor, MI: Servant Publications, 1991.

Townsend, John. *Hiding from Love.* Colorado Springs, CO: NavPress, 1991.

Vine, W. E. *An Expository Dictionary of New Testament Words.* Old Tappan, New Jersey: Fleming H. Revell, 1966.

Yalom, I. D. *The Theory and Practice of Group Psychotherapy,* New York: Basic Books, 1985.

ORDER FORM

Quant.	Item #	Product Name	Price per Item	Total	Info. only (No charge)
	424T	*Building Family Values* textbook	9.95		☐
	424	*How to Build Family Values in Your Church Family* resource packet	79.95		☐
	424W	*Building Family Values* workbook	2.95		☐

Shipping	
up to $3.00: **$1.00**	
$3.01 to $20.00: **$2.50**	
over $20.00: **$5.50**	
Outside USA: Add **$1.00** to above charges	

TOTAL ORDER _____

Shipping (see chart) _____

Amount Enclosed _____

Method of Payment:

☐ Bill Church (established accounts *only*)

☐ Check/M.O. Enclosed   ☐ VISA   ☐ MasterCard

Credit Card Account # ☐☐☐☐☐☐☐☐☐☐☐☐☐☐☐☐

Cardholder Signature _____Exp. Date _____

NOTICE CONCERNING PRICES

The prices shown here reflect the prices at the time this text was printed. Since our resources are printed in bulk and placed in inventory, and prices are subject to change over time, the current prices may differ from what is listed here. Please confirm the prices at the time you order.

Check One:

☐ Pastor   ☐ Youth Pastor   ☐ C.E. Director   ☐ Layperson   ☐ S.S. Teacher

Name _____ Church _____

Address _____ City _____

State _____ Zip _____ Phone _____

Payment must accompany order unless your church has an established account with Church Growth Institute.

Please allow 2-3 weeks for delivery.

Send order to:

Church Growth Institute

Providing Practical Tools for Growth
P.O. Box 4404, Lynchburg, VA 24502

ORDER FORM

Quant.	Item #	Product Name	Price per Item	Total	Info. only (No charge)
	424T	*Building Family Values* textbook	9.95		☐
	424	*How to Build Family Values in Your Church Family* resource packet	79.95		☐
	424W	*Building Family Values* workbook	2.95		☐

Shipping	
up to $3.00: **$1.00**	
$3.01 to $20.00: **$2.50**	
over $20.00: **$5.50**	
Outside USA: Add **$1.00** to above charges	

TOTAL ORDER _____
Shipping (see chart) _____
Amount Enclosed _____

Method of Payment:
☐ Bill Church (established accounts *only*)
☐ Check/M.O. Enclosed   ☐ VISA   ☐ MasterCard

Credit Card Account # ☐☐☐☐☐☐☐☐☐☐☐☐☐☐☐☐

Cardholder Signature _____Exp. Date _____

NOTICE CONCERNING PRICES
The prices shown here reflect the prices at the time this text was printed. Since our resources are printed in bulk and placed in inventory, and prices are subject to change over time, the current prices may differ from what is listed here. Please confirm the prices at the time you order.

Check One:

☐ Pastor   ☐ Youth Pastor   ☐ C.E. Director   ☐ Layperson   ☐ S.S. Teacher

Name _____ Church _____

Address _____ City _____

State _____ Zip _____ Phone _____

Payment must accompany order **unless your church has an established account with Church Growth Institute.**

Please allow 2-3 weeks for delivery.

Send order to:

Church Growth Institute
Providing Practical Tools for Growth
P.O. Box 4404, Lynchburg, VA 24502